Rave Reviews for
Screwed in Business

Phenomenal work! At last someone had the courage to tell it like it is...so much needed in the business world. Most people flirt with investing and entrepreneurship because they get lured into the hype about easy Money and Riches but as Marlene puts it; "Those newbies coming along in business tend to believe that business and entrepreneurial success is a breeze, a cakewalk....Not so! The road is wrought with harsh lessons on money, people, and how to conduct oneself in business."

This book is not to be taken lightly! This should be the bible of what not to do in business and should be on the nightstand of every entrepreneur and business owner. Again, Kudos to Marlene Green for telling it like it really is!

Elmer Diaz, President of the
National Real Estate Investors Association,
www.GuruElmer.com

***

As someone who runs a multi-million dollar a year business, I understand how it's easy for others who lack integrity to try to screw you over! If you want to avoid being screwed in your business, then read and absorb the ideas in this brilliant book by my friend Marlene Green! Her book should be required reading for anyone in business!

James Malinchak, "The Big Money Speaker™",
One of America's Most Requested Speakers
Co-Author, Chicken Soup for the College Soul
www.BigMoneySpeaker.com

***

Marlene Green's "Screwed in Business" is a must read for anyone who is looking to grow their business fast while saving tons of precious time and money. The advice in this book is candid and helpful; I wish they would have made this required reading when I was in law school! –

Nick Nanton, Esq. "The Celebrity Lawyer"
www.CelebrityBrandingAgency.com

***

As a physician, therapist and business advisor, I've personally seen hundreds of business betrayals with my clients and have experienced several of my own. Marlene Green tells the truth about how betrayals are created in business without apology. She boldly discusses the "Dark Side" of business relationships that's naively ignored by most business owners.

Screwed in Business delivers a sobering, practical and

extremely valuable checklist and necessary advice for managing business relationships and deals. This is not an academic book. It is clearly written by someone who understands 101 ways you can get Screwed in Business! Read this book now to prevent unnecessary trauma and financial problems in your business relationships.

Dr. Ernesto J. Fernandez, DOM, AP, LMHC

Physician, Consultant

www.RecoveryfromBetrayal.com

***

"If you have any desire to make a lot of money, help a lot of people, and take a lot of time off, then this book is for you! Marlene Green has carefully woven 101 power-packed points into the body of a masterpiece. Seriously...with so many mediocre business books on the market today, it's a breath of fresh air to finally read someone who is HONEST about the way things are and how to be successful without getting taken for granted. My personal favorites are numbers 1, 7, 11, 20, & 70. I daily see bank-account-exploding results from following these strategies! You're just going to have to get this book and read them for yourself."

Ed Rush

Fighter Pilot, Speaker, & Author

www.EdRush.com

***

"A book filled with great advice, some common sense and some pure genius. Read this and get the tools to avoid becoming one of the millions "Screwed in Business"

Rob Lambert, Esq

OneMinuteRob.com

www.AssetProtectionCorp.com

***

"Sound, honest and experienced advice is hard to find but Marlene Green bears it all to help her readers and friends avoid business disasters that await everyone around every corner. Save yourself some time, money and headaches following the simple but important business nuggets she shares.

J. W. Dicks, Esq.

Dicks & Nanton Law Firm

www.TheBusinessGrowthLawyers.com

***

"Screwed in Business" is a very useful tool for the new and/ or frustrated entrepreneur. I read this book and could relate with just about every one of these problems – especially #'s 17, 34, 42, and 62! In this book Marlene shares fantastic tips... and the lessons she learned on how we can avoid –or-- fix these challenges without wasting anymore time or energy. It's a good read, and I got a lot out of it!"

Craig Valine, "The [Former] Struggling Consultant"™

www.TheFormerStrugglingConsultant.com

"Very rarely do you find a book that is as clear and to the point as "Screwed In Business". This book is chock full of easy to understand principles that can save you money and most importantly your sanity. I only wish that I had access to this wisdom when I first began in business. There is no need to learn from the school of hard knocks when Marlene Green is willing to give you a graduate level course in real world business without the pain."

Robert E. Estupinian CME, MBA, JD.
Certified No BS Advisor
San Jose -Silicon Valley GKIC Insider's Circle
www.GKICSanJose.com

✳✳✳

"Like Marlene, I thought that "they" (professionals I hired) wouldn't screw me over and that "they" supported my dreams and goals. But when I did get screwed, I was pissed and swore that it would never happen again! Marlene made me realize that there are not many people out there looking out for MY best interests and that I have to REALLY do my homework to hire the right people.

Reading "Screwed In Business" was a wake up call for me and even though I have gotten better at handling my business affairs, I realize I still have a lot of things I could 'tighten up.'

"Screwed In Business" made me realize that I can't be so trusting. I've got to do my homework and not be intimidated because that person is a lawyer or accountant. After all, I'm paying them! As Marlene says, "Be clear about what I want and communicate what will MAKE ME happy!"

Shimoda, Celebrity Jewelry Designer
Art for the Soul
www.Shimoda-Accessories.com

✳✳✳

"Talk about a great book on how NOT to get screwed! Marlene's got it covered when it comes to helping you avoid the B.S. of 'getting screwed in business, real estate, life, you name it. Great job, Marlene!"

Bart Smith, Author of B. S. The Book
www.BreakThroughBS.com

✳✳✳

"Love this book! I have been in business a long time and can assure you that I saw myself and everybody I know in business experience these reality checks and harsh lessons. Every successful person I know in business gets their butt kicked at some time so heed these lessons. Marlene really tells it like it is! Well Done!

Jim Connelly, Chairman & Co-Founder
of Integrated Communications Services
Former General Manager of
The Regency Beverly Wilshire Hotel
http://www.onemoresunset.com/

✳✳✳

"For more than 43 years, I've worked with some of the largest companies, corporations, and associations around the world, helping them operate their businesses more effectively, more efficiently, and more profitably. And I've trained hundreds of consultants to do exactly what I do.

"If I would have had the information Marlene Green so plainly and so clearly reveals in 'Screwed In Business', my job would not only have been easier, but the results I've gotten for my clients and the consultants I've trained would have been multiplied several fold.

"It's practical, it's relevant, and most important, it's useable... and that's what makes it so valuable. Get this book. Read it, devour it and above all, implement what you'll learn. It will make all the difference in the world to your business!"

Martin Howey
Founder and CEO
TopLine Business Solutions
www.TopLineBusinessSolutions.com

✳✳✳

"For more than 43 years, I've worked with some of the largest companies, corporations, and associations around the world, helping them operate their businesses more effectively, more efficiently, and more profitably. And I've trained hundreds of consultants to do exactly what I do.

"If I would have had the information Marlene Green so plainly and so clearly reveals in 'Screwed In Business', my job would not only have been easier, but the results I've gotten for my clients and the consultants I've trained would have been multiplied several fold.

"It's practical, it's relevant, and most important, it's useable... and that's what makes it so valuable. Get this book. Read it, devour it and above all, implement what you'll learn. It will make all the difference in the world to your business!"

Martin Howey
Founder and CEO
TopLine Business Solutions
www.TopLineBusinessSolutions.com

✳✳✳

Most people are just way too trusting and feel that nothing bad can happen to them in business. "Screwed in Business" is a comprehensive collection of many of the pitfalls that every business owner needs to be aware of to save ourselves pain, aggravation and financial loss that can so easily happen in business. You just don't realize what kind of problems can come up until it's too late! Read this book to learn about the many pitfalls in business before you fall into a hole yourself!

Sydney Biddle Barrows, Entrepreneur
Author, "Uncensored Sales Strategies"
(co-authored with Dan Kennedy)
Customer Experience Consultant
www.SydneyBarrows.com

✳✳✳

It's hard for me to pick which of the items were most powerful. As the owner of several multi-million dollar businesses, I have experienced all of the painful wounds Marlene discusses in "Screwed In Business". At various points in time over my last 20 years of being an entrepreneur, I have experienced all 101! Wish I had this book to read 20 years ago. Marlene's advice is killer!!!

Richelle Shaw, Entrepreneur
Author, "How to Build A Million Dollar Business
in Las Vegas , without the Casinos"
www.RichelleShaw.com

***

Often we lose sight of what business is for: making a profit. Marlene has laid out foundational wisdom you can use today to create greater satisfaction and profits from your business while you avoid losing your shirt to employees and vendors, and losing big due to your own ignorance and lack of experience. Heed these reality checks as they will save you hundreds of hours of frustration and lost profits.

Otto Ruebsamen
Cash Flow Automator
www.RealEstateBusinessWealth.com

***

Marlene Green can always be counted on for her no nonsense approach to business. She has outdone herself this time in her "tell-all", frank style. If you're serious about avoiding business pitfalls, you need to read this book.

Nina Hershberger
Author of *Creating Customers for Life*
Creator of direct mail phenomenon: The Wallet Mailer
www.Wallet-Mailer.com

***

Do your "future self" a favor and don't just read this book... absorb it! Marlene's message - like a lighthouse giving hope in a sea of voices drowning us with advice - will illuminate a path to confidently protect yourself, your business and your dreams. My advice: Do not do business with anyone before you send them a copy of this book! Let it stand as a beacon to set the standard; help your partners, investors, vendors and employees know what NOT to do...and let them know that you know what to look out for too! So do your "future self" a favor and don't just read this book... absorb it and share it!

Ryan Garey
Idea Machine and "The Couch Coat Guy"
www.RyanGarey.com

***

If you're looking for real world business advice from someone who has 'been there and done that' then look no further. Marlene Green is an astute and seasoned business woman and real estate investor with many valuable lessons to share laid out in a clear, easy-to-read format in this book. This is truly a case where you will profit from her mistakes! A must for every entrepreneur and start-up.

Susan Berkley

President, The Great Voice Company,

Author: "Speak To Influence: How to Unlock

The Hidden Power of Your Voice."

www.GreatVoice.com

***

SCREWED *in* BUSINESS

101 Reality Checks

. . . and Harsh Lessons Learned in
Business that Cost You a Ton of
Money, Waste Your Time and
Drain Your Energy

(Heed these Warnings to Save your Sanity...)

by Marlene Green

Limits of Liability/Disclaimer of Warranty

This book and the information contained herein are for information purposes only. The author, publisher, and copyright holder make no representation or warranties with respect to the accuracy, applicability, fitness or completeness of the contents of this book. They disclaim any warranties (expressed or implied), merchantability, or fitness for any particular purpose.

The author, publisher and copyright holder shall in no event be held liable for any loss or other damages, including but not limited to special, incidental, consequential, or other damages. As always, the advice of a competent legal, tax, accounting or other professional should be sought.

The author, publisher and copyright holder do not warrant the performance, effectiveness or applicability of any sites listed in this book. All links are for information purposes only and are not warranted for content, accuracy or any other implied or explicit purpose. All rights reserved.

No part of this book may be reproduced or transmitted in any form by any means, electronic, mechanical, photocopying, recording or otherwise, without the prior written permission of the publisher.

Throughout this book trademarked names are referenced. Rather than putting a trademark symbol in every occurrence of a trademarked name, we state that we are using the names in an editorial fashion only and to the benefit of the trademark owner with no intention of infringement of the trademark.

This book contains material protected under International and Federal Copyright Laws and Treaties. Any unauthorized reprint or use of this material is prohibited.

This book may be purchased for educational, business or sales promotional use. For more information, visit www.ScrewedInBusiness.com and click on the link for Special Market Sales.

ISBN 978-0-9818274-0-7

Printed in the United States of America

Library of Congress Control Number: 2009933420

Copyright 2009 Screwed In Business LLC. All Rights Reserved

Published by Screwed In Business™ LLC

Book and cover design by Darlene and Dan Swanson of Van-garde Imagery, Inc.

Dedication

To My Dear Grandmother, Francella McKenzie,
who I love and appreciate with all my heart.
Thanks so much for taking care of me throughout
my entire life and being there for me always during my
ups and downs. I love you so much for your many daily
prayers, words of wisdom and encouragement.
I am blessed to always have you in my corner.
Love Always & Forever!

Acknowledgments

I have been truly blessed to have crossed paths with some absolutely phenomenal people throughout my entire life. I can't name them all but below I will name some of the folks who have influenced me the most and who I must express my appreciation and gratitude to here and now.

Your name is mentioned here because of something or many things you have done or said to make a huge positive impact on my life where I felt fortunate and truly blessed to know you.

To My Grandma, thanks for your love and for always being there for me.

To My Aunt, thanks so much for being an awesome role model since childhood and for always reminding me of my strong roots and our rich Jamaican heritage.

To My Mother, thanks for all that you do and your kindness.

To My Cousins, Ashley and Camille, I love you both and am really proud of you!

To My Big Sister, Beverly, thanks for always lending an ear and being such a Rare Gem! I will always appreciate and love you for all that you do, including your great Jamaican cooking!

To Russell Malone, thanks for ALWAYS making me laugh during the best and the worst times.

To Ronald Duguid & Ricardo Keppard, thanks to you both for your friendship and support through thick and thin and for always challenging me to be better and do better.

To All Members of the Glazer-Kennedy Insider's Circle (GKIC) Manhattan & Northern NJ Chapters who enthusiastically show up to our monthly meetings to exchange ideas on entrepreneurship, business and marketing to gain your Slight Edge, thanks for the emotional reward of seeing each of you progress in your business and life endeavors when you take action. (Bravo to you for being smart enough to stay plugged in to GKIC, The Place for Prosperity!)

Thanks to My Great Friends and Business Associates who provide words of encouragement and great support in so many ways, especially when it was most needed: Rama Duvvuri, Michael Najair, Richelle Shaw, Robert Morales, Ed

Rush, Nick Nanton, JW Dicks, Howard Zeiden, Renee Duff, Bart Smith, Jordan McAuley, Dr. Ernesto Fernandez, Barbara Spinks, Kimberly Burleson.

Thanks so much to Darlene & Dan Swanson for getting this book's cover design & layout done as promised in record time and not screwing me in the process!

Much Appreciation goes out to my Absolute Favorite Entrepreneurs, Marketers, Mentors and Real Estate Teachers for generously sharing your wisdom and expertise and being such Great Teachers, Philanthropists and Role Models. The astute readers of this book will Google™ your names to learn more about you!

To Peter Fortunato, Jack Miller, John Schaub, Jack Griffin, Louis Brown, Sherman Ragland, Dyches Boddiford, David Lindahl, Robyn Thompson, George Ross, and Elmer Diaz, thanks for sharing your wisdom and experience about how to really build wealth with real estate and how to protect it.

To Dan Kennedy, the Napoleon Hill of the 21st Century, thanks for taking your precious life time to produce such a large body of work for entrepreneurs and business owners serious about learning direct response marketing and becoming true Renegade Millionaires. I am still working my way through all of your writings and desperately trying to keep up. And Yes, I am thrilled to be part of YOUR "Herd."

To Bill Glazer, one of the most brilliant business men and marketers on the planet. Thanks for _**always**_ pointing out where the money is in everything for those who really want to find it and get it!

To Eben Pagan and Alex Mandossian, you are both simply the best on the planet at teaching entrepreneurs how to live their best life while being a great leader. Thanks so much for all your work, wisdom and in-depth research that helps entrepreneurs perform at their very best in all areas of their business and personal lives.

To Nido Qubein, Joel Osteen, Frank McKinney, Sabrina Lamb, Scott Sullivan, Susan Taylor, Terrie Williams, Vince Zirpoli, Jim Connelly, Wyatt Woodsmall, Muhammad Yunus, Jim Rohn, and Bill Phillips, thanks for demonstrating to me how to live a life of significance and leave your mark on the world by touching people's lives and making a difference for others in your own unique and powerful way.

To Joe Polish, Jay Abraham, Paul Colligan, Martin Howey, Jeff Walker, Rich Schefren, James Malinchak, Brendan Burchard, Clate Mask, Scot Martineau, Nina Hershberger, Yanik Silver, Mike Stewart, Jim Edwards, Dr. Ed Hallowell, Chris Hurn, Armand Morin, and Rick Raddatz, thanks for being such brilliant marketers and entrepreneurs who also know how to really have fun while doing business.

To My Favorite Business Moguls of All Time, definitely worth studying closely, thanks for being such great role models and leaving clues in your writings and life's work on how to create phenomenal success and lead an extraordinary life: Richard Branson, Oprah Winfrey, Al Neuharth, Donald Trump, Gene Simmons, Linda Johnson Rice, Russell Simmons, Tyler

Perry, Norm Brodsky, Ted Turner, T. Boone Pickens, Michael Masterson, MaryEllen Tribby, Earl Graves Jr., Robert L. Johnson, Joseph Sugarman, Guy Kawasaki, Ephren Taylor, and Butch Stewart.

SO THERE YOU ARE AND BRAVO TO YOU ALL FOR BEING A POSITIVE INFLUENCE AND SUCH A MAJOR BLESSING IN MY LIFE! THANK YOU.

Contents

Introduction

We must learn from the mistakes of others.
We can't live long enough to make them
all ourselves.

— Anonymous

First of all, who am I to tell you about being screwed? Well, I have lost a ton of money because I trusted others too much, I got into business deals that just didn't work out due to circumstances beyond my control (like the local economy), I signed personal guarantees that I got called on, I wasn't paying close attention to business expenditures, and I took my money for granted and allowed other people to spend it freely.

I have been involved with lawsuits and been through litigation with unscrupulous parties who were former friends and business partners.

I have also wasted time with attorneys and lenders who burned through my money and time at will.

I have dealt with a handful of wacky customers who did a 180 degrees on me when they weren't happy and I have dealt with tenants who seemed like the nicest people on the planet and then don't pay their rents and do serious damage to my property.

I have dealt with building contractors who saw me as a big green dollar sign and stole as much money as they could by spending on extra materials, doing shoddy work, and draining my time and energy by causing me much stress.

I have also screwed myself because I was just way too trusting and gave people the benefit of the doubt and simply did not know how to quickly say NO or HELL NO!

Why do I write this? Because no one talks about the lessons learned from the bad stuff that happens to us in business. Newbies coming along in business tend to believe that business and entrepreneurial success is a breeze, a cakewalk.... Not so! The road is wrought with harsh lessons about money, people, and how to conduct oneself in business.

I write this not to complain, be negative, or gain pity, but to share some of my lessons learned in business the hard way. Heck, I was warned by my elder mentors about several things and still I ignored their wisdom because I never thought that bad things could happen to me and I paid greatly in lost time, lost money, wasted energy and lost relationships.

In my dark and quietly desperate times of trouble I did a lot of searching for solutions and guidance and found little out there on how to deal with bad stuff like getting screwed in business! Not too many people will honestly talk about the really bad stuff that happens to them in business because it's embarrassing and there is fear of being perceived as negative and a failure.

So, I thought that after being in business for almost 20 years, I would share my experiences and what I have learned from others so that perhaps you will be wiser than I was and heed the warnings and learn from the experience of those who have gone before you, versus first-hand personal experience. You may disagree with some of my conclusions but at least you are aware of the issues that may arise and how to deal with them.

Life is a journey filled with ups and downs. Read the bios of the most successful entrepreneurs on the planet. You will realize that none of them ever said it was easy and all had to deal with drama and trauma. I have provided a Reading List from my personal library for you at the end of this book.

I know you will identify with some of the lessons I share and I encourage you to post how you have gotten Screwed in Business, what lessons you learned, and what wisdom you would like to impart to others on our website at www.ScrewedInBusiness.com for the benefit of others in my audience.

There you will realize that no matter what your story is, you are actually in the majority of business owners and entrepreneurs, and if you have been ashamed, embarrassed and quietly beating yourself up, just stop right now! Sometimes life throws us curve balls...but we all must bounce back!

A Word of Caution
From The Author...

"Work hard on the job – you get paid. Work hard on yourself, you get a fortune" – Jack Griffin

This book is <u>not</u> about you being a helpless victim to getting screwed by others in business. It is about taking precautions to protect yourself before getting into various types of business transactions. Below are 7 Tenets that you must keep in mind as you read this book:

1. Don't continue to play the role of victim and blame others for your troubles though they may have indeed screwed you. If you continue to play victim, you are giving up your power to the perpetrator. Take full responsibility for what happens to you and recognize that you are in control of changing your situation, no matter how dire. Just DO SOMETHING productive every day to get out of your bad situation, including asking for help and walking away to start over and pursue a totally new venture.

2. You really have no control over other's actions and behavior, so don't be surprised at what people will do or say to screw you. You can only act on those things that you have control over.

3. Invest your time wisely every day as only your daily activities will determine your future success or failure.

4. There is no time for self-pity. (OK, maybe just a little bit if you just lost a million dollars and your precious time spent has gone down the drain!). Do your best to snap out of it and focus 100% of your time on finding solutions and digging yourself out of the deep hole you may be in.

5. No matter how bad things get, make a daily commitment to improving and constantly working on yourself in all areas of your life: Your Health, Your Diet, Your Mental Health, Your Relationships with Friends and Family, Your Business Skills and Education (including Marketing, Sales, Copywriting, Finance, Leadership, Management, Technology and Client Relations).

6. Stay away from negative people and those who don't support you! Surround yourself with people who uplift your spirits and encourage you to pursue your endeavors, despite your setbacks and failures.

7.   Most importantly, no matter what business you are in, make a daily commitment to <u>Being of Value to Others</u>! As long as you are of value to others and offer more value to others, <u>you will always prosper</u> no matter how much you got screwed in business!

101 Reality Checks and Harsh Lessons Learned...

*Once you know what you want – know why
you want it. With a strong enough why, you can
endure any how.*

— Anonymous

How We Get Screwed by Employees, Professionals, Vendors and Other Service Providers

It's better to look ahead and prepare than to look back and regret. - Bits & Pieces

1. Set ground rules and be very clear upfront as to how you want to do business with everyone. If you don't, you are subject to whatever they throw at you and however they come at you and that will waste your time, money and energy...GUARANTEED.

    Before engaging anyone, be very clear and put in writing what will make you really happy and what you expect them to do for you. So many times when I have hired assistants, web designers, contractors and other help, I shot myself in the foot and had a date with disaster because I was not crystal clear about what I wanted for myself and then communicate that to them! You have a disaster in the making and much time lost if you don't have clarity and set your ground rules up front with everyone.

Now when I hire contractors, aside from having an agreement or contract with them, I take time out to review my Wish List and the "What will Make Marlene Really Happy" List. Works wonders for setting expectations!

2.   Respect your money....if you don't, others won't! Nobody will ever value your money and appreciate what you had to do to earn it more than you will.

In many instances when I have entrusted others to oversee receivables or take care of expenditures, I later find out that there was money left on the table, money was wasted, or they overlooked some detail that proved to be costly to me.

You must take time out to keep track of your money on a daily and weekly basis in both your business and personal lives because it is very easy for things to fall through the cracks. Don't trust that others are paying attention to monies owed to you, charges that haven't gone through, or savings that you are entitled to.

Always count your money personally before it's too late! If you lose track weeks, months or years later, it is hard to recoup your losses and of course, no one but you is responsible! It's also very painful and time-consuming to try to audit the money trail after a long period of time has passed.

Never allow anyone to sign checks for you. When business owners and entrepreneurs are too busy to pay attention, trusted partners, trusted employees and trusted managers can easily embezzle funds from their companies.

You must always keep your eyes open and protect your assets and your nest egg by being educated and informed. Ever so often, carefully audit your books; get to know the vendors being paid, and what you and your business are paying for on a regular basis.

3. Never assume that someone who presents him or herself as an upstanding professional is one. They must prove themselves at least three times before you can provide a recommendation and put some, never all, of your faith in them.

It is critical to allow anyone who works with you time to show what they are made of. So many of us who hire team members and vendors become enamored and never allow them time to really prove themselves to us first!

With regards to hiring, you must hire slowly (and fire fast). Use a process called Topgrading by Brad Smart of www.SmartTopGrading.com and consider personality tests like www.Kolbe.com to really make sure you do a thorough evaluation before bringing folks on board to work with you.

Smart has an alarming formula that allows us to calculate the Cost of a MisHire. It is a reality check for business owners and entrepreneurs as to how important it is to be thorough when bringing people on board to work with you.

Top grading® ➤ **Cost of Mis-Hires Form**

Job title of person mis-hired or mis-promoted: _____

Dates person was in position: from _____ to _____

Reason for leaving:
❏ Quit   ❏ Fired (or forced to resign)   ❏ Transferred   ❏ Demoted
❏ Retired   ❏ Died   ❏ Other

1. **Total costs in hiring the person:** $ _____
    - Recruitment/search fees (any guarantee? if so, was money recovered?)
    - Outside testing, interviewing, record checking, physical exam
    - HR department time and administrative costs (for all candidates)
    - Travel costs (for all candidates, spouses, other executives traveling to meet candidate)
    - Time/expenses of non HR people (all candidates)
    - Relocation (moving household goods, purchasing house for candidate)

2. **Compensation: (sum for all years person was in job)**
    $ _____
    - Base ($ x number of years)
    - Bonuses ("signing," performance, etc.) for all years
    - Stock options (realized for all years), benefits (insurance, 401k, etc.), car, clubs

3. **Maintaining person in job: (sum for all years person was in job)**
    $ _____
    - Administrative assistant for all years
    - Office "rental" (incl. electricity, etc.) for all years

- Furniture, computer, equipment, travel for all years
- Training
- Other "maintaining" costs

4. Total severance: $_____
- Severance fee (salary, benefits, use of office), lawyer fees
- Outplacement counseling fee
- Costs in lawsuits caused by the person (EEOC, harassment, EPA, OSHA, etc.)
- Administrative costs in separation, wasted time of people in separation

5. Mistakes/Failures, missed and wasted business opportunities:
   (For example... drove a key customer away, impaired customer loyalty, launched three "dog" products)

6. Disruption: $ _____
   (Costs of inefficiency in the organization, lower morale, lower productivity, impaired teamwork)

7. Other: $ _____

8. SUM OF ALL COSTS (#1 through #7): $_____

9. Estimated Value of Contributions of the mis-hire: $ _____
   (Even if a $50,000 per year store manager drove away customers and stole $1 M, perhaps he contributed something — hired five excellent employees, came up with a merchandising idea worth $500K per year to the bottom line.)

10. NET COST OF MIS-HIRE (#8 – #9): $ _____

"WASTED" Hours:

   Number of additional hours spent dealing with mis-hire's weak points — patching things up with customers, etc.

www.SmartTopgrading.com

4.   Don't be intimidated or impressed by Attorneys, CPAs, Realtors, Lenders, and Mortgage Professionals who present themselves as experts. Again, they must deliver the goods through your entire client experience with them for you to do business with them again.

I have been burned by Attorneys and CPAs who just want to get their fee upfront and do little, Realtors who just want to have you sign the Listing Agreement (and then they disappear), and Lenders who blow you off after they get your business. It is critical to pay attention to your entire customer experience: before, during and after you engage with these so-called professionals to see if they are worth recommending or worth doing business with in the future.

Visit www.MarleneRecommends.com to check out my good friend Sydney Biddle Barrows' book and her program called "XXX Rated Sales Strategies" where she talks with Marketing Guru, Dan Kennedy, about Sales Choreography and delivering a great Customer Experience in any business.

5.   Know that with 97% of business owners and professionals, they assume they gotcha because they made a sale or had you sign an agreement and got your money. They don't realize that this is just the start of determining whether or not they have made one sale or have a client for life!

We all need to be cognizant of this: Are you making a sale to get some instant money or to get a client for life? Always remember that your goal should be to get a customer, get a member, get a client or get a patient that you will nurture for the long term. It's all about long term relationships. Too many business owners and professionals operate with a Hit and Run strategy!

As the client, you need to be very clear as to why you have hired any vendor or service provider and set clear expectations as you what you hope to get from them upfront!

In real estate, I have had really bad experiences with contractors when I just assumed that they knew what to do and would "take care of me". Boy, did they take care of me by doing shoddy work and stealing materials. Sadly, I can only count on one hand the contractors who I would gladly work with again!

I learned really quickly the importance of setting expectations and then inspecting what I am expecting along the way. You just can never assume that people will do right by you!

6. Inspect what you expect. Never get comfortable and assume that any service provider or professional is doing right by you and looking out for your best interest...this goes for all Contractors, Vendors, Attorneys, CPAs, Lenders, Mortgage Brokers, Realtors, Employ-

ees, Sub-contractors, Virtual workers, Creative Professionals.

The people who truly care about having you as a client for life are few and far between!!! I can count on one hand, the service-providers who I have dealt with who I truly feel valued me as a client and care to do their very best for me and my business. By the way, these people are the ones who I refer and will do business with again because they have earned it by consistently over-delivering in my experience with them.

7.   Pay close attention to the true motivation of so-called coaches, experts and mentors! They can't guarantee your success, only you can, but I have observed that many only care about the money that they will get from you and that's it.

Those are the folks who are very attentive BEFORE they get their hands on your credit card but then you can't get them or their staff on the phone after the charge clears. Pay close attention and watch out for that. If necessary, get feedback from others and check references. Follow your instincts and if you get a bad feeling, don't do business with them.

On that same note, I have invested in educational materials and services from people who I don't care for or who I find cocky. Why? Because the value of the information they offer is so damned good!

Know when to focus on the Message, not the Messenger.

8. If you are not happy with the performance of a service professional, vendor or contractor, let them know upfront. When you allow mediocrity or non-performance to continue and linger, it ends up costing you 1000 times more because of time lost, energy wasted, money spent, and the hassle of starting all over again.

    Everyone can identify with the endless stories of having to hire 2 or 3 contractors before finding the right person to complete the job...or being on your third Realtor because the first two tied up your property with 90 day listing agreements and produced no results.

9. Marketing guru, Dan Kennedy says, "They All Go Lame" - So true, because most people work on a daily basis to get money now. They are not looking for a long-term relationship and will just do whatever is needed to get by. You can hardly rely on them to do what they agreed to do and deliver as promised from start to finish. Therefore, don't be surprised when they go lame on you. Accept it and just move on.

    Be pleasantly surprised when they hang in there with you for the long term and do an outstanding job. Take care of those people who are Loyal "A" Players because they are truly hard to come by.

10. No matter their position, take care of those who take care of you and treat them with respect. Ever since I entered the workforce as a high-school intern, I was always conscious of treating everyone around me with respect – including blue collar workers – from sanitation workers, restaurant staff, bathroom attendants, office-cleaning workers, secretaries, city employees, check-out persons, bank tellers, security guards, building superintendent, and property maintenance personnel. This also applies to general contractors and those sub-contractors who perform with excellence and do a great job.

   Never turn your nose up at them because you do need them to get things done and meet your goals. Despite what you may think, what they do is indeed valuable and of importance in the grand scheme of things.

   Everyone brings value to the table or else they shouldn't be there. As a leader, if people sense that you don't value them, you will have problems.

11. Never advance money to ANYONE for services to be delivered. You will never see it again if they flake out on you! If they ask for money upfront before services are delivered, go elsewhere. I have experienced this with virtual assistants, web masters, attorneys and building contractors.

   There is the rare case where materials are needed upfront. Fund only that...but NEVER PAY for services not rendered no matter how good the story is! Truly professional service providers know how to structure things so that they can deliver for the client and then get paid for work done.

Even while writing this book, I foolishly broke my rule and made an exception by paying a graphic designer money upfront because I knew the person well and he said that he was almost done completing my project. Turns out that he only got my project to 95% completion and then came back to ask for 50% MORE money to get it done many weeks later past our agreed on deadline. This was blackmail since he knew I really wanted to be done with the project. This was a harsh reality check for me and I ended up having to get the job done elsewhere because I didn't appreciate my project being held hostage. Bottom line, never advance money to ANYONE for services to be delivered. Pay them only AFTER the job is done.

12. Be cautious of retainers, especially when it comes to attorneys! I have paid retainer money that has been burned through by attorneys on 'Research", "Phone Calls", "Email", and everything else except getting the results that they were hired for in the first place.

I had one Englewood Cliffs, New Jersey attorney who got $2,500 upfront retainer money for 4 months and didn't do any work on my case justified by a ton of excuses (dog died, vacations, daughter getting married, out sick, etc.). He even fired himself by saying he had a lot of personal issues to deal with and was very sorry. He then promptly refunded a paltry $177.36 of the retainer money. My new attorney was horrified that his predecessor kept the money, wasted my time over many months and did nothing! Hmm, is that called theft?

Though I have friends I respect who are attorneys and having an attorney is in many cases a great insurance policy, I must vent a bit here: I have had attorneys who I have hired voice their opinions about my business and investment decisions and offer unsolicited opinions about my dim prospects for future success!

NEVER allow any attorney to step out of line and get away with voicing their opinions on your business strategy, marketing strategy or business acumen. They are totally out of order for doing so! They seem to feel that because you have a legal problem and have come to them for help they can say whatever they want and get away with it. Remember that their sole purpose is to make sure you are legally protected and are aware of all your legal options. They are not there to give business or investment advice.

I will give some leeway and listen to an attorney who is also a seasoned entrepreneur or experienced residential or commercial real estate investor, but always remember that attorneys tend to be very conservative in terms of risk-taking and not very creative. Bottom line, be wary of advice you get that is outside of that professional's area of expertise and competence!

13. Take care not to allow any professional that is earning big commissions or fees on your deal to be learning on your dime. You get the short end of the stick, pay dearly in time, and don't get the benefit of their experience because they don't have any.

These professionals I refer to include realtors, attorneys, mortgage brokers, accountants, financial advisors and any type of consultant. Your best bet is to deal with pros who have been around the block, have seen the ups and downs and have lots of war stories to share. They are bringing the value of their wisdom and experience to the table.

To determine who the pros are, listen for war stories, case studies and stories of past clients and situations as a clue.

As an example in real estate investing, you can always tell who the seasoned landlords are when you can swap nightmare tenant and contractor stories with them.

14. If you find yourself educating or informing any service professional who is supposed to be providing a service for you such as a realtor, mortgage broker, technology

consultant, attorney, bookkeeper, executive assistant or accountant, STOP and go find someone else.

It is a big waste of your time to be doing this and you gain nothing from it, except that they will want to hang around you some more, to learn more, as the clock ticks!

Hire experienced, confident, knowledgeable folks, though likely at a higher fee, to get your work done fast and benefit from the added value in experience that they bring to the table for you.

15. Place on your calendar when things are due to you and by whom. Funny how time flies when you entrust your business or financial affairs to others and you get so busy, it's too late or you lose a ton of time (that can't be recouped) before you realize that they haven't been on the ball or haven't been taking care of your business.

If you have a lot of things going on in your business, monitor what deliverables are owed to you using deadlines and get a daily status on them. Also have a weekly status meeting on all projects with your team. Never wait longer than a week to get the pulse on your business or projects.

16. When dealing with any kind of transaction, especially service providers, ask upfront what all the fees and payments are required to do the deal so that you don't

overlook anything and will budget accordingly. I am always amazed at how people sneak line items in during a transaction and expect you to accept it because you are committed and have time invested with them.

Make it clear upfront what your budget is and that approval is needed before additional charges are incurred.

17. Never assume that people have or get the same vision that you have set forth for any project. No matter how much you describe your vision and big picture goals, don't assume that everyone is on board or that everyone gets it.

Listen to what they have to say and observe what they do as time passes. Action speaks louder than words.

As a Leader, you must never stop driving home to your team, the Vision, The Mission, The Purpose, The Core Values and the Objectives for your organization.

18. Always get agreements and price quotes in writing up front. You will be amazed at the misunderstandings that take place when things are done verbally. All agreements must be in writing with deliverables clearly stated, pricing clearly stated, milestones clearly stated, and deadlines clearly stated.

19. Think twice about paying ahead on certain services.

Sometimes you forget about them because the money is already spent and life happens.

Manage your cash outlay by paying as you go and consuming as you go. If you are not using those services then you should cancel them and save your money.

I have paid ahead on gym memberships, real estate services and internet memberships and haven't used them because I forget about them! Yes, this has been one of my short-comings and I have wasted a ton of money here! Save your cash for something you are actually using where you will get a return on investment and you are sure you will use it.

20. Always ask probing questions when you are about to hire a so-called expert or professional. Get them talking by asking a ton of questions because this is the only way for you to find out if they really are expert at what you are hiring them for.

This especially applies to folks where you have time and a ton of money on the line with them, like attorneys, contractors, mortgage brokers, lenders, realtors, accountants, inspectors and technical consultants, like webmasters.

Listen closely to how they respond to you – do they get defensive or insulted that you question them? Do they brush you off? Are they impatient? Can they cite past projects, past clients, best practices, lessons learned? Do they sound like they have your best interest at heart in terms of providing solutions that will help you reach your goals?

Anyone worth their salt and wanting to build a relationship with you and get your business will take the time to respond accordingly. If not, follow your instincts and don't hire them.

21. Never get cozy with staff or employees. They are only in it for what they can get and most don't truly embrace and share your dreams and business goals. Most are in it only for a paycheck! After-all, everybody has to eat and pay bills, right?

As a business owner or entrepreneur I strongly recommend you read Dan Kennedy's No B.S. Ruthless Management of People and Profits. This book honestly lays out the harsh reality of being a business owner and the fact that your goals are totally different from that of your staff or team members.

Some people may find this harsh but the truth is that the people who work for you are primarily there to get a check so that they can live their own lives and take care of their bills. At the end of the day, your business is not their number one priority. Always remember that everybody looks out for Number 1 first!

22. Test people on small projects and opportunities to

see how they perform and conduct themselves before exposing them to bigger projects and greater responsibilities. You will save yourself much grief and heartache when you find out sooner rather than later that you don't care to work with them!

I experienced this first hand when I was considering bringing on a webmaster from a friend's company to work with me. He seemed reliable and loyal until I found out that he was a convicted felon and that he went berserk and sabotaged my friend's company website, stole money from the company's bank account because he had their PIN numbers, and blackmailed the owner of the company for money.

My friend was at this webmaster's mercy because he entrusted the webmaster with his entire technology operations and had no documentation or backup resource to go to. Though this true story is a bit extreme it speaks to the importance of carefully doling out responsibility to those who work for you and having a backup plan if things go awry and they look to screw you or the company.

How We Get Screwed By Friends and Family

Of that which nothing is known, nothing can be said. — Ludwig Wittgenstein

23. If someone is truly talented and a pro, but a bit rough around the edges, give him/her feedback just once and see if they take action on your advice. If they don't, it's not worth your time trying to help them out further.

    I had a really talented member who was an athlete that served the corporate market and was eager to get more clients. He was smart and really talented but did not dress well enough to attract more corporate clients. After all, first impressions are really important.

    I pulled him to the side and told him that he has everything going for him, except for his attire, and just needs to work on that. Lo and Behold, he was highly offended and stopped attending my meetings! It's unfortunate because he missed out on many opportunities to get more clients simply because of his ego or just being totally clueless!

    I often wonder if it was worth the time for me to

give free advice to him... and it obviously wasn't because it was not taken as something of value! Perhaps I should have charged him for the advice, then it would be considered valuable!

24. Take heed not to get into any business partnerships with ANYONE you would like to keep as a friend. I still have yet to be able to identify a long-term business partnership that has worked out successfully amongst friends or members of a peer group of any kind. It is funny how greed, envy and jealousy intensify among former friends when business and money matters just don't work out.

    Strong emotions take over and it is quite the energy-drainer! Life is too short to be in battle with people you used to like and have good times and good laughs with!

    Yes, I know that you may know of many successful business partnerships amongst friends but I am willing to bet that those are few and far between.

25. Note these words of wisdom: "Keep your friends close and your enemies closer" – I have observed that it is your closest friends, family and key employees who can do the most damage to you and/or your business. They have insight into your operations, they have seen you with your guard down, and they know your weaknesses.

It's sad but true that in today's world you can never let your guard down 100%. You just never know who in your inner circle has it in for you and what motivates them. Be on the alert and never be surprised if people turn on you or stab you in the back.

Sadly, your closest confidantes and those who surround you daily are the ones who can do the most damage and will seek to use all they know about you against you if things go south. Don't be shocked and surprised, just plan accordingly and expect that much.

I agree with Donald Trump when he says "Trust No One". Of course that is easy to say in a sound bite but hard to live by. So just be careful.

The reality is that it takes time to find out who you can trust and who you can't and you cannot go through your entire life not trusting anyone. The only thing you can do is be alert, protect yourself, and not be surprised when people pull a Dr. Jekyll and Mr. Hyde on you and seek to screw you over! This is guaranteed to happen to you in business at some point in time.

26. Pay close attention to how people around you handle things when it is a bad situation. Do they bail out when things get bad? Do they hang in there and fight with you? Do they let you take all the bullets? Do they leave all the work for you to do? Do they empathize with you? Do they offer help, support or advice?

The best time to find out about the true nature of folks around you is when things go bad. You will be in for some surprises about people's reactions and behaviors, but pay close attention and learn by observation as things play out.

You will easily identify who is loyal to you and in your corner and who is not!

You will also know how to deal with everyone when you bounce back from the bad situation.

27. More words of wisdom: My good friend Ronald Duguid always says "A tree never changes its roots" – At the end of the day, liars will be liars, thieves will be thieves, angels will be angels, and the Good Samaritan will be the Good Samaritan.

I honestly don't think that people really do change or operate differently when put under pressure or are in a bad situation. They will revert back to what has always worked for them: Liar, Thief, Angel, Good Samaritan.

When Ron shared this with me years ago, I used to argue with him and give folks the benefit of the doubt, but as time passed I realized that he was right on the money! "A tree NEVER changes its roots!"

28. Words mean nothing. Judge people by their ACTIONS ONLY!

29. Never assume you know what's going on in people's lives, whether things seem to look good or prosperous for them, or things look really bad. You just never know what's going on behind the scenes or in their heads.

  If you really want to know, just ask. Never make sweeping generalizations or assumptions as to what is going on with folks. Notice how surprised we are everyday when we hear shocking news about regular folks or a celebrity gone berserk. Many of us assume that all is well with them, their health, their relationships, and their business. You just never know!

30. Sam Cooke sang: "Nobody wants you when you are down and out..." Yes, when people perceive that you have nothing of value to offer OR that there is nothing there for them to get from you...they disappear. However, when you seem to be successful and well-connected, many are drawn to you.

  People are fickle. I say that we should be confident, yet humble, and recognize that most people are not around you because they LOVE you and think the world of you. They are around because of what they can get from you and what you can do for them. Never forget that.

  Sounds harsh but it is true...Consider all the celebrities who fall from grace or 'nice' people you know who grow old lonely, or who die alone, or who are alone sick in the hospital, or even those who have a small turnout at their funeral. Gee, where is everybody? Where are the adoring fans, friends and family?

31.   People are always down on what they are not up on! Take any critics' comments with a grain of salt.

Use your own judgment and do your own research before coming to a conclusion. Be wary of The Critics in your industry as they may lead you astray.

Be immune to criticism when you get wind of gossip, rumors and harsh criticism of you or your business activities. Simply do your best and strive for excellence.

32.   Jazz Guitarist Russell Malone says, "When you are not appearing you are disappearing." Never go into hiding, whether business is good or bad. Exposure will ultimately lead to opportunities. Always be somewhere and out doing something if you are truly a marketer of your business. Frankly, everyone in business should be a marketer first so you must always be appearing somewhere, in print, online, at an event...be somewhere.

33.   Pay close attention to how people perform and behave AFTER they think they have made the sale. Some people will do a hard sell and chase you down to close a deal but once they think they gotcha, you can't hear from them!

Big mistake on their part as they think you are not paying attention to the fact that they have not delivered on what they promised.

34. Pay attention to how people do business, especially service professionals. Are they organized and efficient in dealing with you? Are they learning on your watch or do they bring value and expertise to the table? Are they just kissing your ass while being incompetent? Are they sloppy in their paperwork and presentation? Pay close attention so that you can decide if they need to be fired or if you should do business with them again.

35. Get an attorney to review all agreements in the beginning of any transaction or engagement, even those which seem simple and harmless. It sucks when bad things happen and a situation arises later on that you did not address in your agreement and you have to waste time and money dealing with it and getting an attorney involved.

36. In all business engagements, have clearly written terms of engagement discussed upfront and signed off by everyone so everyone is aware of where you stand. Take no shortcuts here as it will come back to bite you.

How we Get Screwed Out of Our Time and Expertise

Don't let your expectations get ahead of reality
— Jack Griffin

37. Watch your time and value your expertise and knowledge! Don't go about spending your time freely or dishing out all of your expertise and knowledge to anyone. I have done this to my detriment over my entire career.

    What happens is that, when free, the valuable information you share with everyone to encourage them or connect the dots for them, is never appreciated because they didn't have to pay for it – as you might have.

    So, they don't covet your advice. If they paid a couple of hundred or couple of thousand dollars for the same information, then they would value it more. Don't EVER waste your time spilling your guts! If you do after reading this, you REALLY don't value your time or expertise.

    Friends and family are the worst when it comes to

not appreciating your advice and counsel so don't be surprised if they blow you off. Again, this goes back to "Familiarity Breeds Contempt"!

38. When people want to pick your brains, they are picking your pocket. Don't subject yourself to brain-picking sessions at breakfast, lunch or dinner, unless you are the charitable type and you honestly feel the person is really deserving of your time.

In most cases, when folks "pick your brain" they have no respect for you or your time and discount the value of the ideas, information and resources you have shared with them. Protect your time and charge for it when strangers want to pick your brain!

If people you just meet start saying that they want to "get together to pick your brain" – state your consulting fee. Remember that your time is your most valuable asset. If you allow anyone to "pick your brain" understand that they are "picking your pocket" and stealing your precious time!

Watch out for the email requests, quick phone calls, voicemail messages, and being cornered at a meeting. Those are the times to be on high alert for your brain to be picked! Master the art of the great escape by simply walking away, stating your consulting fee, stating your boundaries publicly, or just saying NO.

I know of one famous marketing guru who is a

master at disappearing after he does a seminar. He is consistently gone in the blink of an eye as soon as his presentation is done! There is also a multi-millionaire developer who when he has fund-raising events at his home, literally drives away with his family as a signal to all guests that it's time to go and the event is over. I am amused at how these successful people have mastered the art of the great escape.

I have never gotten a good return on investment of my time when I allowed someone to "pick my brain", EVER! I have spent hours on the phone and in person dispensing valuable free advice to people I just met and have nothing to show for the time spent. Don't subject yourself to this because you will regret it!

How We Get Screwed in Business Transactions and Real Estate Deals

Heaven has no rage like love to hatred turned.
Nor hell a fury like a woman scorned
— William Congreve

39. Don't personally guarantee bank loans where if things go south all of your personal assets are on the line! I have heard so many real estate gurus talk about this and did not heed their warnings. Sure enough, things went south on one of my projects and creditors came to collect all of my personal stuff. Talk about a dose of reality!

Let's face it, many entrepreneurs and investors are very optimistic but frankly you just never know what will go wrong. There are so many disasters that can happen to affect your business and investments that are out of your control, like 9-11, the economic downturn, lawsuits, and business partners trying to steal from you.

So, the lesson learned is if you are going to personally guarantee anything, you must have a gazillion back up plans and contingencies in place and know what to do if things don't work out as planned! You also want to have an asset protection plan in place before you do so.

Always know upfront what you are going to do if things don't work out as you planned. This is absolutely critical in all of your personal and business affairs!

Most institutional lenders want a personally guarantee and it's perfectly within their right to want this, but you as an entrepreneur should understand the consequences of a personal guarantee. Having all your personal assets seized, your credit scores quickly going south, dealing with collection calls from creditors, and waking up to frozen bank accounts is the beginning of a really dark period in your life and it's definitely not worth losing everything you have worked so hard for just to do a business or real estate deal.

It is critical for you to learn how to conduct business and finance your operations without ever having to sign a personal guarantee. These include getting private lenders who you can work with, having equity participation in your deals, and just being relentless about running a profitable business where you are making sales and getting to cash so that you never have to borrow money from an institution and risk signing your life away.

40. Understand that the IRS and Creditors never go away. So, if you haven't paid your taxes and the IRS or some

other arm of government comes knocking or you have creditors trying to collect because a project went south on you, do what you can to buy time and come up with a game plan to deal with them.

Make sure you understand what your rights are and what the end result of their actions will be. Be proactive in coming up with a solution. Don't blank out in thinking that they will go away and ignore their efforts to get all that you have! Just know that they are relentless and determined to collect.

Most importantly, get experienced legal counsel to guide you. Also recognize that you are not alone and that millions of people in the past have gone through these bad experiences and got through it with their sanity still intact. They became wiser and stronger and moved on with their lives by putting the past behind them.

Also, having gone through such unforgettable financial dark periods in your life forces you to make smarter and wiser financial and business decisions in the future. Just know that it is possible to rebuild because your life is not over, even though you may feel like it is.

41. Before you get into any business transaction with anyone, make sure you have a clear understanding, on paper, as to what each party's roles, responsibilities and expectations are. Most importantly, have a very clear exit strategy if things don't work out! Without a clear

exit strategy, when things go wrong, or if there is a misunderstanding, emotions take over. Both parties lose and the legal system and the attorneys win.

The last time I found myself sitting in my litigating attorney's office talking about a lawsuit that I had to file against a former business partner who sought to steal a property we controlled together, I learned that we never had an exit strategy in the form of a "Buy-Sell Clause" that helps us dissolve the partnership. It became quite costly and I swore that before I got into any deal ever again, I would have several exit strategies to get out, whether things went well or had gone bad! Don't ever forget to be clear on your exit before going into any business or real estate deal!

I will also add that you must always use an attorney when going into partnerships and any legally binding arrangements. Never play attorney and try to use the paperwork from a course or book without a local attorney reviewing the paperwork. Always get an attorney licensed in your state to create or review your documents thoroughly. Love them or hate them, Attorneys are the best and cheapest insurance you can ever have when it comes to legally binding arrangements.

Remember, ONLY the Attorneys win when you have to go to court to fight a legal battle! Totally not worth it and litigation should be avoided at all costs.

Also realize that it is the raw emotion of anger and

outrage that drives us to go to court. Honestly though, it is far wiser for us to look at the value of our time and what we end up with even if we "win" a legal battle and the judge rules in your favor. You may get a judgment and then can't collect on it. Most times, you will find out that it is not worth it to go to court.

That said, I must admit that there is something to be said for the emotional satisfaction of challenging people in a legal forum when you have been wronged by them! Just think twice about whether or not it is worth it to spend your precious time doing so.

42. Never put your finances or credit on the line for anyone. There are many horror stories of spouses' credit scores and financial reserves being depleted because of their spouse's indiscriminate behavior when it comes to fiscal responsibility.

Same goes for family members, children and close friends. Just say no. They will find another way if they want it badly enough!

Never sign on the dotted line and take on debt for the benefit of anyone else, unless you are prepared for the possibility of loss. I have consistently seen where family members, spouses and business partners get into trouble because their relative, spouse or business partner who they thought they could trust to be responsible flakes out on them or things simply did not work out as planned.

If you choose to disregard my advice, be ready to accept losing –big or small-and please don't be shocked and surprised, start crying, or get angry. You were warned. Your money and your credit are too valuable and sacred to be placed in the hands of others without careful consideration of the risk you are taking. Protect your finances and your credit.

People who borrow your money or credit can be fickle and when pushed to the limit they are only concerned about self-preservation and not about their relationship with you or how you see them. Just be aware of this.

43.   Never loan money you can't afford to lose or write off. I still have yet to have loaned money to anyone where I didn't have to ask them for it since the time passed for them to pay it back, or I had to pursue legal means to get it back. You will always be made out to be the bad guy because you asked for your money back so your rule may just be not to loan money you can't afford to lose or do without.

Know that folks are great at coming up with excuses as to why they can't pay you back your money or meet their obligations to you. Heck, they may even be valid and honest excuses. Just be ready for this and have a back-up plan so that you are not left in a deep hole you can't get out of because you didn't get paid back.

Life happens and you always have to have cash reserves and a backup plan to take care of yourself. You absolutely cannot leave your fate in anyone else's hands and be at the mercy of others' actions and decisions.

44. I am very much anti-partnerships because I have gotten burned badly a couple of times, partly because I blinked, trusted too much and was gullible! However, joint ventures I would carefully consider. Still, be sure to make sure roles, responsibilities, and expectations are clearly spelled out on paper and that your exit strategy is clear if things go south. Also, in real estate pay attention to who controls the money and the title to the property, preferably you or an entity you control.

   Most importantly, take a really hard look at the personalities involved and be honest about whether or not you want to do business with them. It's easy to get in but hard to get out when things go awry with partners!

45. Never go into a transaction or deal with only one exit strategy. Always have at least 3 exit strategies and always ask yourself what you will do if things go south or if the other parties flake out.

   Also ask yourself what will come of your reputation if you flake out or things take a turn for the worse for you where you can't meet your commitments. These are critical questions to ponder before getting into any business engagements or costly entanglements.

46. I have heard real estate guru, Ron Legrand say: "Avoid Costly Entanglements!" This is seared into my brain. In business and life, we must truly consider the downsides of anything you get involved with because when things go south you will forever be kicking yourself for not being more careful and thoughtful.

47. Pay close attention to how people behave or respond when things don't go quite as well as planned with any venture. If they start to retreat or get greedy or envious, take note and be ready for the storm. People's true nature comes out when things go bad or the road gets rocky.

48. Be careful about getting into projects where there is a disproportionate balance in terms of who is doing the work, while all are reaping the rewards.

I was an investor in a project with seven partners and things went south very quickly when only certain people were pulling their weight and others did not. Also remember that you can only have one leader, not seven! Remember: "Too many cooks spoil the broth."

49. Be clear that if you enthusiastically take on all the work in a group project, where everyone benefits, no one will argue with you or go out of their way to contribute or lighten your load!

Folks who volunteer for boards, for their church, or for other non-profits can really identify with this as they end up sacrificing much time and energy and eventually burn out. It's good to contribute your time and energy to a great cause or project but just take caution not to over-commit yourself, and then become resentful, and ultimately burnout!

50.   If you are going to get a mentor, which you should, find a mentor who has done exactly what you want to do and who will never compete with you, steal your ideas, disrespect you, or be threatened by your success.

How We Get Screwed by Clients and Customers

If you give me six lines written by the most honest man, I will find something in them to hang him.
— *Cardinal Richelieu*

51. Know that Familiarity Breeds Contempt!!!! When people get close to you and you let your guard down they start to take liberties and take you for granted. It's best to stay at arms length with most everyone and be very careful who you let into your inner circle. This applies in both business and social environments, especially when dealing with employees, vendors, clients, prospective customers and business colleagues. Set boundaries with everyone and don't allow them to cross the lines with you.

   Stay at arms-length with everyone that you do business with because if they get too close, they get comfortable, they get sloppy, and they start to take shortcuts. Happens every time, GUARANTEED.

   Always make sure everyone knows that you expect the best from them and to be treated with respect...

and that you will do the same for them. I have never ever seen anything good come out of becoming too chummy with employees, clients, customers, members, patients, vendors and service providers. Maintain your boundaries. If you don't you will regret it!

I always wondered about the quote "Familiarity Breeds Contempt" and why it exists. It exists because it is **ALWAYS TRUE** in both business and personal relationships!

52. People have very short memories when it comes to the good things and favors you have done for them. They have very long memories when they feel they had a bad experience.

I am sure you have been generous with your time, money and resources and then you later find out that these are taken for granted and not appreciated by the other party. Don't be surprised when this happens. It's just human nature and we have to go into relationships knowing this.

I say still be generous but don't expect anything in return from anyone, including close friends and family members. Just be pleasantly surprised by those few who truly appreciate you and express their gratitude to you.

Many people don't realize that it costs nothing to simply say Thank You!

53. People also have very short memories when it comes time to return a favor or show gratitude. They have very long memories when you refuse to compromise or do their bidding.

    You must remain within your integrity and have clarity about what you will and won't do. In all dealings with people, always follow your gut and instincts... they are usually right!

54. Be very selective about who you invite into your home or personal office. Your surroundings send a message and people will judge you or make a determination of who you are and what you have by your surroundings. They may be wrong or they may be right. Bottom line is that this process will happen in their minds unconsciously and you will be subject to their assessment of you, good or bad, as time passes.

55. As the leader of any group or organization, never allow anyone to disrupt the group or poison the well for others with their negative commentary and attitude. You will lose good people who are easily influenced and it is a disruption to the spirit of your organization, whether a non-profit or for profit.

    Don't ever think twice or delay in getting rid of any detractors. Get rid of any rotten apples or negative people who come around you immediately. Don't ignore early clues such as what they say, how they say it, and what they do. Follow your gut and your instincts, always and do pay attention to the rumor mill.

I experienced this in an organization I ran. Everyone seemed happy but once a couple of negative people came around their negativity spread like a cancer and I had to get rid of them once I verified that the cancer existed.

As a leader in your business or any organization, you must be ruthless and quickly get rid of those who detract from the higher purpose of the organization or seek to poison the minds of others because they have some ulterior motive or they are simply unhappy and negative people.

If you delay on rooting out evil or cutting out this cancer, it will overtake your members, your staff and ultimately your entire business.

When anyone is a vexation to your spirit, immediately get rid of them, ask them to leave and part company. Don't delay. Things will only get worse!

56. Give a 100% refund to get rid of trouble customers or clients and send them on their way. Life is too short to deal with people who are an aggravation. I love what Marketing Guru, Dan Kennedy says, "If I think about

them 3 nights in a row and I am not sleeping with them they gotta go!"

Also, have a clearly stated refund policy in place upfront so that if there are problems no one can try to make up their own terms or policy for you or negotiate with you.

57. When it comes to money and clients, provide a written and detailed accounting of all monies so that when there are charges and refunds it is clearly explained and documented for them.

58. Don't extend credit, especially to those you are just starting to do business with. There is no relationship there and it's easy for them to walk away owing you money.

I have had this happen several times and literally lost thousands of dollars because I was too accommodating with folks. Make sure to collect your money upfront or nicely decline doing business with anyone who can't pay your fee for services delivered.

How We Screw Ourselves...

In order to have more - do more. In order to do more - become more. — Jack Griffin

59. Accept that you can't do it all yourself! You need an experienced, talented, loyal and committed team of people around you to get things done. These people can be part-time, full-time, local, out of town, virtual, outsourced, employees, vendors, contractors, family members, partners, or professionals in various specialties. No matter what your situation is, you need help.

So many business owners and entrepreneurs screw themselves and burn out by trying to have their hands in everything, become an expert in everything, and do everything. We must learn the art of delegation and only focus on our unique abilities and talents - what we do best. I learned this the hard way by trying to do everything myself and learn everything and got burned out fast.

I didn't want to take the time to learn how to hire and manage others and I didn't think anyone could do it like I want it. Now granted, when you bring others on to work with you, you must manage them for results, and because you are dealing with human beings, you have to accept that you must learn and master the Art of Leading and Managing others. You must also inspect what you Expect and Have a System of Monitoring the Details in your Business.

If you are serious about enjoying the rewards that a successful business or real estate investment will bring you, like a better lifestyle, more money, and free time to enjoy what you really love, then you need to bring skilled and talented people on board to operate your business. Look behind the scenes of your favorite entrepreneurs, investors and business owners and you will see a team of people who help them make things happen.

It does take a mindset shift to accept this reality and it is best for you to figure this out sooner rather than later and stop wasting your time and energy. You may be at a stage where you feel that you don't have enough money to bring people on to work with you but you must make it a priority to at least have a highly capable personal assistant to take care of the things you are doing that are not the highest and best use of your time. This will free you up for growth and working on activities that bring in more money and profits.

You might even start by having people come on board with you on full sales commission, unpaid internships, or part-time help a couple of hours per week to start. Well structured bartering of skills and resources is another way to get started if you have no money for salaries.

Visit www.MarleneRecommends.com to get some resources from one of my mentors, Vincent Zirpoli, on instituting a Performance Management System and a Strategic Management System in your business.

60. Don't allow people who are working for you to dump monkeys on your back. This is when they constantly bring back problems and issues for you to solve. This means that you don't have a system, you did not train them properly, or you hired folks who don't know how to solve problems and bring value to the table.

    You know that you have the monkey problem when you are stressed out before getting into a conversation with this team member because you will come away with more work to do and more decisions to be made. Master the art of delegation and Master the skill of hiring people who take pride in being creative problem solvers and look to make themselves more valuable to you in executing on their responsibilities without your constant input.

    As a business owner and entrepreneur, it is worth taking time out of the daily grind to automate and systemize repetitive work that needs to get done by your team members in all areas of your business. I highly recommend a lifesaving tool called Infusionsoft that small businesses around the world are using to automate their business processes so check out my comments about it at www.MarleneRecommends.com.

It is critical for you to get clarity about your specific business goals and have measurable objectives for your own sanity and the benefit of your team members.

61.   Learn to say NO easily and quickly. This goes for those of us who say YES and kick ourselves when we are overwhelmed or can't deliver because we have agreed to unnecessary obligations to other people. Practice saying NO with confidence and no guilt.

62.   Don't play fetch for anyone. This is when people who you don't know and who are not your clients make requests that you need to go "fetch" for them. This puts you in a state of being obligated to cater to people at their whim. If you have resources to share on an ongoing basis, set up a place for them to go fetch it themselves.

63.   When people perceive that you are in a position of influence or can do things for them, they will be bold enough to ask you to do favors for them just because of who you are. Have no problems saying "NO", "Not Yet" or "I can't help you."

Recognize that many folks expect you to nicely go

out of your way for them just because they asked. Don't fall for that or else you end up screwing yourself royally!

Always do things on your own terms and on your own schedule. Don't fall victim to other people's agendas.

64. If you show any signs of lack of confidence or low self-esteem, people will knock you down and take your lunch money!

In life in general, exude confidence, even if you don't feel so confident.

If you don't, your enemies and detractors will promptly start chipping away at you.

Your attitude about your bad situation is everything! If you are upbeat and just smile as you roll with the punches you will feel much better and people won't mind being around you. Do this while working on rebuilding your business and making your comeback.

If you have a bad attitude and a foul disposition, no one will want to be around you. Remember, at the end of the day, no one really cares about your misfortunes in business because they are already caught up in the drama of their own lives. Being bitter and angry and expending negative energy is really a waste of your precious and limited life time.

65. If you can't deliver on something, be upfront and let the other parties involved know what's going on. The

worst thing you can do is lead everyone to believe you have it covered and let them have false expectations of you. It's better to come clean upfront by communicating honestly. It is also mental freedom for you!

66.   Watch out for folks who can't differentiate between business and friendship and seek to get a break or a pass. In the past when I have gotten into business entanglements with business colleagues who I consider friends, they EXPECT to be treated differently and don't feel that they are subject to constructive criticism or your expression of concern when things aren't going well. Even when they do something wrong or don't deliver or meet their obligations, they expect you to turn a blind eye. Again, don't mix business with friendship!

67.   When you have gotten screwed more than once, consciously lay down your ground rules to everyone in writing and keep a rulebook so that everyone is forewarned that you are fore-armed and won't tolerate any crap from anyone!

Here is the document I provided with all my contractor agreements when hiring real estate contractors called "Marlene's Ground Rules":

✻✻✻

14 GROUND RULES FOR DOING BUSINESS WITH US, YOUR CUSTOMER

Based on years of experience we find it necessary to document our expectations upfront so that you know what we expect and we can both start off on the right foot.

We only deal with Professionals. If you are serious about doing a professional job and providing excellent service you will read the following and abide by these guidelines. Some have followed these ground rules and have been rewarded, and unfortunately many haven't.

1) Are you a True Professional? If you are not, don't bother starting this job!

2) Time is Money...Don't waste our time or our money; and we won't waste yours.

3) Respect our Time as we will Always Respect Yours.

4) Follow up when you say you will. If you don't, you won't hear from us again.

5) Be on time. If you can't, call to notify us as soon as possible; not at the appointment time. Don't leave us waiting. We will pay you the same courtesy.

6) Be honest and upfront about what you can and cannot do and what resources you have. Don't come to learn on the job on our time.

7) Communicate any concerns or difficulties you may have with us or the job sooner rather than later. Don't lead us on a wild goose chase and waste our time, money and/or energy. Be upfront and don't keep us in the dark. We don't like surprises and we do respect your opinion even if we disagree. If there is something that we have overlooked or could do better in your professional opinion, let us know; after all, you are the professional!

8) Don't even try to take advantage of us...We will figure you out sooner or later...likely sooner, and cut you off. Don't lie to us or steal from us. We won't let you off the hook and you will pay for your deception.

9) Do your job professionally and efficiently...that's why you got the job and will be paid promptly for the job.

10) Do Quality work. We will hold you to it.

11) If you make a mistake, fix it. Don't try to justify it or deny it.

12) Don't bring your ego, personal problems or issues to the job. You are here to provide a service or a product that solves our problems, as the Customer.

13) Actions speak louder than words...We judge you by your actions.

14) Provide Excellent Service even AFTER you get paid.

Earn our respect as a Customer and we will become LIFETIME RAVING FANS and repeat customers and be honored to serve as one of your referrals.

© Marlene Green, Your Paying Customer

***

68. Until you value your expertise, knowledge and time enough to <u>charge</u> for it, no one else will value your expertise, knowledge and time enough to <u>pay</u> for it.

69. Test everyone when they least expect it...you will find out who is in your corner and who isn't.

70. Trust no one and have a high degree of paranoia. Yes, there are absolutely wonderful professional people out there, I know many. However, maintain high standards and don't ever accept mediocrity.

Pay close attention, even after the deal is done to

how closely they pay attention to detail, how thorough they are, how they communicate verbally and in writing, how they handle your money, your staff and your clients, and how they take your deal all the way to the very end.

71. When things go bad it does no good to allow yourself to become paralyzed into doing nothing through Fear and Sleepless nights....nothing is accomplished by being fearful or worrying. It's best for you to DO SOMETHING to change the course of things and take some kind of corrective action on a daily basis. Fearfulness, Making Excuses, Blaming Others, Whining, Complaining and Worrying solve nothing.

Always remember that we live in the land of opportunity and you simply need to get busy pursuing new opportunities to rebuild after getting screwed. Most importantly, never forget the lessons learned in getting screwed and the people and circumstances involved with those lessons. If you forget the lessons, you are bound to make the same mistakes again.

72. Never spend 100% of your time on just one project or fighting one battle. Problem is that things may not work out as you planned and you will have just invested time that you can't recoup into a lost cause. The high price is the opportunity cost of all the other things you

could have been doing that would have had a high return on your investment of time.

I learned this the hard way when I spent 100% of my time over 3 years of my life focused on one project which I expected to pay off big. This did not turn out as planned. It was financially devastating because I did not pay attention to other opportunities that would have paid great dividends. I did not divide up my time for various endeavors. The opportunity cost is in the millions.

What I have learned is that it's best to diversify and not put all your eggs in one basket. Though you need to diversify, you must also stay focused and not be scattered having your hands in too many projects. You must strike a balance between diversification and focus.

73. Never assume that all the folks around who look happy, well-off, and successful truly have their stuff together and all is perfect in their lives! I have come to find out that there is likely a lot of STUFF going on that's kept private like family issues, money problems, health issues, mental issues, etc. Bottom line is to be grateful for your blessings and to keep pushing forward. Things could be much worse!

I have been privy to the private lives of some seemingly successful people and have been surprised to learn of their insecurities, low self-esteem, short-comings and challenges they have in their personal relationships.

Frankly, no one is perfect or has the perfect life. Everybody is screwed up or has short-comings in some area of their life!

My dear grandmother always says never envy people for what they have because you don't know how they got it. You also never know what demons they are fighting and what they *really* did to get their possessions!

We mentally screw ourselves when we are occupied with the lives of other people as opposed to focusing on what we can do to improve our own lot in life.

74.   Never allow accounts receivables to pile up over time. You are losing money everyday when you don't collect promptly and you in effect become a creditor.

Also, keep timely and impeccable financial records. If you don't, you lose track and there is no exact accounting for inflows, outflows and cash flow in general.

Business owners who don't put a financial and accounting system in place upfront are destined for frustration, sleepless nights and wasted time trying to get a handle on their financials. This is important not only for tax purposes but also for proper fiscal management of your business. You owe it to yourself to watch your cash flow and money management.

75.   Be careful about spending your time freely enriching others – to the detriment of your own business affairs.

It is just people's nature to take what they can get from you if you choose to give it freely.

Several years ago I happily volunteered for a non-profit and spent all my time working on their cause at the expense of my own business. I was so excited to help but placed myself and my business at risk.

The lesson learned from this is that you must take care of yourself first before you can save the world. Some people may call this selfish but you have to make self-care a priority because you can't help anyone for too long if you are weak and don't have a solid foundation to operate from.

76. Always best to hire a project manager or operations manager to handle the details of any project you are working on. You then oversee the manager. It is a downward spiral when you get involved in the minutiae and details of your business that don't generate revenues and is not the best use of your time.

Only spend your time on the things that generate the most revenue and the things you do best. It is said that you should spend time strengthening your strengths, not your weaknesses.

I have wasted a ton of time, money and energy trying to oversee details I am not expert at when it was best to pass them off to someone else and do what I do best.

Chances are the people you delegate or outsource to will do it much better than you ever could...you just need to give them clear instructions on the results you want and inspect what you expect them to do.

77.   Your time, not your money, is your most valuable asset! Once time is spent you can't get it back! The 2 best books on the planet to read regarding how we spend our time are: The 4-Hour Work Week by Tim Ferriss and No B.S. Time Management by Dan Kennedy.

Read those 2 books and your whole outlook on how you spend your time and your life will be changed forever! Get them and read them NOW. Also, visit www.MarleneRecommends.com to see some other great resources on proper Time Management and Business Management.

Also, check out The Power of Full Engagement by Tony Schwartz that addresses Energy Management and Eben Pagan's Wakeup Productive program. My reviews are available on www.MarleneRecommends.com.

78.   Keep things simple and don't complicate. When you complicate things, things move slowly, don't get done and everyone remains confused. Simplicity with Speed is the way to go!

One of my favorite entrepreneurs who is great at keeping things simple, yet elegant, is ultra-luxury real estate developer, Frank McKinney. Check out his books like Make It Big, The Tap and Burst This which explain how he gets so much done by keeping things simple while paying attention to details daily, staying focused, and closing the loop on things.

I also urge you to support his Caring House Project Foundation which builds homes for the desperately homeless in Haiti and elsewhere around the world. Visit www.CHPF.org.

79. The devil is truly in the details. Though you must get things done quickly, make sure all the mission-critical "make or break" details are being handled properly as there may be holes in your business or sales process. This applies to everything from buying real estate, to creating multi-step marketing campaigns to sell your products and services, to the sales process experienced by your prospects and clients.

Again, check out books and resources including those by Dan Kennedy and Sydney Biddle Barrows on www.MarleneRecommends.com that give you guidelines on plugging the holes in your leaky sales and marketing bucket. The lack of Following up is one of the biggest problems facing businesses, both large and small, and ultimately leads to business failures due to loss of prospects and customers over time.

80. Be immune to criticism as people casually criticize using generalities or specifics. Don't ever take it personally. Just shake it off.

　　Bottom line is that life is a journey and there are ups and downs. We all just need to make the most of the journey and deal with things as they come up. Also, nobody is perfect!

81. It is a waste of energy to complain and whine. For the most part no one cares about your drama or troubles. Only a handful of people – family and close friends – will listen. You just have to deal with whatever issue is on the table and handle it as best you can. If you need help or advice ask, but don't just complain for the sake of complaining. Complaining solves nothing.

　　Reality is that no one cares! Everyone is preoccupied with their own drama and troubles and don't care to hear yours!

82. At times, on first meeting you, people may underestimate what you know, what you can do and who you know. Never try to impress them. Use their misjudgment to your advantage by continuing to astonish them by just doing what you do extraordinarily well. Your results speak volumes.

　　They will eventually come around wanting to really get to know you. People will always come along with their prejudices and make assumptions about you because of what they see.

You just have to always be true to yourself and never internalize THEIR prejudices, ignorance or shortcomings.

83. Never allow any other person to tell you what you can or can't do. Why should you be subject to THEIR limiting beliefs, limited expectations and limited thinking?

I so often see adults accept the limits others place on them (consultants, licensed professionals, spouses, supervisors, friends, family, coaches, gurus, mentors). Don't ever fall for that! We all can accomplish great things or do things out of the box or in an unconventional fashion once we set our minds to it. Just go do it!

84. Never follow the crowd and do what everybody else is doing! Always do the opposite and do your best. Compete not only against others...but also yourself. Do your very best. Have very high standards and never settle for mediocrity even though you will be criticized by many for having high standards!

85. Aim to be debt free and have more than enough business and personal cash reserves and cash flow to pay for your debts and your lifestyle. The best peace of mind is being debt free and knowing that you don't

owe anyone or if you are carrying debt, having the confidence that you can pay it off on demand. Zero debt is something to aspire to despite what some investors and lenders may say!

86. Keep all your financial and legal documents in order on a daily and weekly basis. The longer things pile up the more stressful and costly it becomes. Take time out to go paperless, backup your files and avoid piles!

   If you don't heed my advice you will add to your stress and experience decreased productivity if you have piles of paper to wade through to get things done or have to search for hours to find things.

   Have offsite backup of important paperwork and computer files just in case there is a fire or disaster where your business is located. Imagine for a second what life will be like if you had no backup of important files or paperwork and the time it will take to recreate all of that!

   Visit www.MarleneRecommends.com to check out some of my favorite time-saving productivity tools and resources.

87. Before going into a business relationship with anyone, test them and pay attention to how they treat others and talk about others who are their peers and who work for them.

This will give you much insight into what to expect from them as you go about developing a relationship with them. Keep your eyes and ears wide open. Their current behavior will tell much about their future dealings with you.

If you go into business with them, understand that people will also judge you based on your association with them.

88.   Know that as you size up people, they are also sizing you up so put your best foot forward and be conscious of your behavior and the impressions you leave behind. Strive to be a welcome guest in everyone's home and a valued colleague in everyone's little black book.

89.   Never engage in gossip and be careful who you voice your honest opinions to! It will likely get back to the person who was the subject of the gossip and be circulated. It's a small world and gossip is a big waste of time and energy.

90.   Keep your business and financial affairs private, no matter the state of your affairs – good or bad. People take great pleasure in gossiping about your affairs but if you share nothing, there will be nothing for them to gossip about.

In addition, never show anyone the whole movie when it comes to projects you are working on and plans in the works! Only show them the end result of your action plan or a clip of the movie, if necessary.

91.   When you are doing well and making money, people will count your money and guesstimate the Gross Amount that they think you are making. They then think that you are swimming in money and will approach you from different angles to get a piece of the action or as I was once told, "Marlene, you gotta share the wealth..."

What they never take into account is your Net Amount...and Taxes. People forget that there are fixed overhead and variable costs involved in every business. They also never take into account that you have worked hard, likely sacrificed much, and made several years of investment in yourself and your business to get to where you are.

They also look at you as an overnight success and one who had it easy to achieve what you have. They don't realize that there were likely many ups and downs, sleepless nights, stressful times, disappointments and much drama on your path to success over many years.

This is why it's so important to read biographies of successful people in various fields. If you pay attention to their journey you will realize that there are all types of experiences along the way that brought them to where they are.

Hone in on those experiences and realize that it

takes preparation, study, trial and error, hard work, perseverance, resilience, a mental commitment to achieve business success, and sacrifice in many areas of your family and personal life.

It is never a cakewalk and therefore it's out of order for people to come along and think they are entitled to siphon off some of your money or steal your time just because you "got it good". This may sound selfish and it is. Self-preservation has to be top of mind always because people will come along, knock you down and take all they can, in a heartbeat!

92. Follow your instincts and gut about people when you first cross paths with them or as you get to know them. Just listen and observe what they say and do. This is critical to your survival and in determining what moves you are going to make.

93. Never allow anyone to ruffle your feathers or see you sweat. Stay calm, cool and collect at all times. Take a deep breath. Smile. Visualize yourself handling things with ease and finesse.

Most of all don't focus on the problem at hand; focus on finding solutions and executing on those solutions.

Have zero tolerance for people around you who only focus on problems and never offer up solutions. They are wasting your time!

94. When anyone is a nuisance or a vexation to my spirit, I literally cut off all communications with them, delete them from my contact list and my brain...and move on with life. I waste no time or mental energy on them or their issues. Life is too short. Spend your time with those who love and appreciate you and all that you do.

    Strive to lead a calm, peaceful life and minimize aggravations because you just don't know how long you have as tomorrow is not promised and we only have the present.

    However, if any party insists on being a serious and damaging nuisance to you like filing frivolous suits, slandering your name, or making false accusations, this is the time to fight back swiftly using everything in your arsenal against them. Never allow anyone consumed with envy, jealousy or greed to get away with attacking you or any of your interests. You must deal on the offensive with people who operate that way.

95. Don't cut special deals or give special breaks to prospects and clients as it will always come back to haunt you in your business. Keep everything uniform across the board and life will be simple.

    When we cut special deals and give breaks to people, they tell others. Everybody will try to negotiate with you and never take you seriously or value what you have to offer.

    Most of all, focus on being of value and over-delivering on value so that no one will even contemplate negotiating with you.

And while you are at it, simply commit to only dealing with people who can afford to pay you. Just go where the money is! Don't deal with Broke People.

96. When things go south with you and clients, creditors or partners, take the initiative to communicate honestly with the other party before bringing on attorneys. If people are honest and reasonable, it can save a ton of headaches and legal fees.

97. Be part of a mastermind group of positive and smart like-minded people and always feed your brain with good stuff. Check out Think and Grow Rich by Napoleon Hill to learn about the Power of a Mastermind. Also, check out www.MarleneRecommends.com for mastermind groups nationwide that you can plug into.

You screw yourself royally when you allow yourself to be brainwashed by the daily news and all the negativity that abounds.

Yes, it's important to face the stark reality of things going on in our country and in our world but you must also realize that you should only focus on the activities that you have control over. That's all you can do.

You must also be nimble and alert enough to adjust as things change in your environment.

Read biographies and magazines like Millionaire

Blueprints Magazine, Inc. Magazine, Success Magazine and Entrepreneur Magazine to feed your mind with great information about entrepreneurship and business.

Visit www.MillionaireBlueprints.com to get your copies of Millionaire Blueprints which gives you Detailed Step by Step Blueprints and Resources from Self-Made Millionaires that you can follow. Become a Member of the Millionaire Blueprints Arena right now and devour all of the issues ever published because you will learn much from the stories of the self made millionaires profiled!

You will also come to realize from reading Millionaire Blueprints that the road that these self-made millionaire entrepreneurs and business owners travel is a bumpy one filled with excitement and lots of ups and downs, but yet they triumph as they reach several milestones and continue on their journey – never giving up.

Also remember that in life you are going to "Attend a Seminar" by either investing in one by choice, or have it forced upon you through the School of Hard Knocks.

Ron Legrand, a well known real estate guru says "You Are Going to a Seminar" when you don't abide by the warnings and harsh lessons learned by those who have gone before. You will jeopardize your success!

Every time you break the rules and buck the wisdom of those who have gone before, you are likely to get seriously hurt in the real world School of Hard Knocks.

Despite the warnings of my mentors in a Private

or Seminar setting I have done things like Signing Personally on really large Notes, Hiring Staff without thoroughly checking them out, and Getting into Partnerships without an Exit Strategy or a Buy-Sell Clause, because I trusted my partner. I think, "Oh, nothing will happen to me, I'm safe" and then things go south and I just screwed myself. Never think that bad things can't happen to you...and that it's only for the other guy.

My advice for you: Learn from the most successful people in your field who are willing to teach and share their wisdom and advice. Abide by their advice and wisdom and be sure to understand WHY they take the position that they do. It is likely that they got screwed by others or screwed themselves and went through the School of Really Hard Knocks.

Understand that there are no free rides and few free passes. Yes, there is a lot of free information offline and all over the Internet, but you must also be willing to take the next step to invest money and take time out of your schedule for your business education and personal development. I see many people waste time and miss out on huge opportunities that would change their lives for the better because they are short-sighted, closed-minded and not willing to invest a little money or time in themselves. That's unfortunate as time waits for no one!

Why not save yourself the trouble and invest in a

course, seminar, coaching program, retreat or boot-camp, versus, being out there on your own trying to figure things out, wasting time with trial and error, and making mistakes? That's just plain stupid!

Visit www.MarleneRecommends.com for my rec-ommendations on really excellent courses, seminars, coaching programs, retreats and bootcamps you may attend depending on your location, interests and busi-ness goals. Remember, Invest in your Lifelong Educa-tion and Always Learn from the Best! I can honestly say that I have NEVER regretted any investment that I have made in my ongoing lifelong learning. I strongly believe in gaining a slight edge by learning and observ-ing from others in many different arenas.

98. Don't ever forget that your primary job is that of be-ing an Astute Marketer who seeks to attract and keep customers, clients, patients, and members. No matter what business you are in, for profit or not for profit, you need to always be marketing to bring people in and keep them. You must have several new customer acqui-sition strategies working at the same time. A business is defined as a collection of customers. No customers simply mean No business.

I was guilty of paying attention to everything BUT marketing to bring in new customers and my business suffered greatly. I was in the majority of small business owners nationwide whose businesses fail because of lack of marketing and undercapitalization. That sucks and is easily remedied with proper planning, seed capital and the right ongoing education!

Lesson learned is to have a marketing plan and always be marketing and promoting everyday no matter how great or how bad things are in your business. Make this your number one priority above all else, always!

Also master the art of selling in person, online and in print. Selling is where the rubber meets the road in business and we are all salespeople, despite what some of us may think. It is easy to say you are too busy, frustrated or overwhelmed to take time out to refine your selling skills and perhaps that is part of the reason why your business has gone south! Always be selling something. I will also add that everyone on your team must consider themselves salespeople.

Don't overlook the importance of being a lifelong student of the art of selling which includes your presentation, positioning, and copywriting skills. Visit www.MarleneRecommends.com for resources to help you with Marketing, Selling and Copywriting.

99. Cash Is King. Positive Cash Flow is Queen. Watch your numbers – ALWAYS, and pay attention to your Cash Flow. Many business owners shoot themselves in the foot by spending their time on everything else and not

monitoring their cash reserves and cash flow. Cash Flow is the lifeblood of any business and something that must never be delegated to others to monitor!

Notice that businesses from the sole proprietor to small and medium sized businesses to huge corporations operate in the red because they just aren't watching the numbers and watching their cash flow. It's just common sense.

I have been guilty of this too because I thought I was just too busy to deal with the numbers. Well, I screwed myself again and oh how painful that was!

I now watch the numbers like a hawk and am ruthless about being profitable. I have learned not to get into any business or real estate deal for ego's sake. It's all about PROFITABILITY! That's the only game we should be playing in business.

100. Seek to develop working assets. I believe in acquiring properties to build long term wealth because it's all about passive and positive cash flow - plus people always need to live somewhere.

You just have to pick the right neighborhood to invest in to have that real estate asset work for you for a long time! I learned this the hard way 3 times in my real estate investing career where I had really nice properties in bad neighborhoods that were either high in crime or had no economic engines at work!

Recognize that both tenants and the investor who will buy from you in the future will also be looking at the neighborhood first before they fall in love with the property. The neighbors, the neighborhood, and the economic conditions of the area are critical factors to take into consideration.

I also believe in developing assets that include intellectual property assets that can be repurposed over and over and will add value to people's lives. Mastering the business of information marketing is also wise no matter what business you are in since selling information and expertise can bring in additional revenues to your business. For more information on the Information Marketing Business, visit www.MarleneRecommends.com.

On both counts, real estate and intellectual property assets can work for you passively and increase in value over time. As long as they are throwing off positive cash flow generated by your stable of tenants and customers, life is good!

101. No one cares more about your business than you could ever so take care of your business, count and watch your money and never take it for granted.

The worse thing ever is to lose money or run out of money because you weren't paying attention and keeping your eye on the ball! Lack of Cash is the ultimate deathblow. Seek to avoid that.

The Bernie Madoff scandal reminds us of 2 things: Always do your Due Diligence yourself and keep tabs on everyone who handles your money and your business affairs. Never Trust Blindly, ever...no matter how smart and sophisticated you think you are.

Model smart wealthy people who own nothing so that others have nothing to take from them if things go south, but they control everything. Learn about asset protection.

If you got screwed, are broke, ran out of cash, or down in the dumps, to make a comeback, commit to value your time and money more and protect them both in the next round! Immediately restrict all cash outflows and expenses to the bare essentials, then simply get to work everyday to bring in money and quickly take whatever action is necessary to make great things happen, again!

Most importantly, take time out to enjoy your loved ones and just to live and enjoy the simple things in life daily. You just never know when your number will be called. Despite all the ways we can get screwed, just keep your eyes open, take care of your physical and mental health, live well, love much and laugh often!

Bonus Chapter

You never go broke taking a profit. - Anonymous

Warning! Watch out for these Real Estate Closing Nightmares...All the things that CAN go wrong that wastes your time, energy and money!

This is an outline of things for you to watch out for and how you as real estate investor and a borrower can get tangled in the web of characters who cost you time, money and energy to get to the closing table...or perhaps never close.

Lender Representative or Mortgage Broker You Have Chosen:

- Interview for experience and verify if they are competent.

- Know who is in charge of their operations.

- Judge if they are a wimpy or a take charge person with a sense of urgency to get to closing.

- Know their fees upfront, documents needed and the timeframe to get to closing.

- Ask what can go wrong, and what the worse case scenarios are.

- Be wary of those who paint a rosy picture.

- They will screw you and take their time after they get your nonrefundable fee so try not to pay an upfront fee.

- Everything is negotiable. Question every fee.

- If the Lender promises a closing tomorrow or next week and the Lender's Attorney is not involved, they lied to you!

- The Lender's Attorney rules and is your ticket to the closing table.

- Watch the dates in your commitment letters.

- If they said funding your deal is a slam-dunk, don't believe it. It ain't over 'til it's over and you actually walked away from the closing table.

- Be honest and upfront about your financials, property values, credit scores, principals, and all parties involved.

Your Buyer or Tenant Buyer

- Prequalify and know all of their financials and skeletons upfront.

- Inform them on how they CAN NOT get to closing so they don't screw up.

Your Seller

- They lie!

- Double Check and do Due Diligence on everything they tell you. Study the history of any property you purchase, including prior owners, if possible. Always buy Title Insurance!

- Ask for all paper documentation on the property so that you don't have to come back to them later: leases, deed, survey, inspections, appliances info, utility bills.

Appraisers

- Give them as much information as you have to help them with their reports and meet them at the property when they go out to do their appraisal.

Contractor

- Keep them informed

- Know what is needed from them: contract, permits, liability insurance

- Don't allow work to go on without proper permits and insurance intact. Remember, you and your company are on the hook and liable if anything goes wrong.

City Officials & Inspectors

- They are Employees with Big Egos & lots of Power who can slow you down. Get to know the players if you are doing Construction work

- Know your Zoning Rules

- Know all the Fees you will be charged for Permits.

- Know what's involved in turning on your Utilities and how much lead time you need.

Title Company

- Get a local title company with an experienced title attorney who does closings on properties similar to yours. This means they can do it in their sleep.

- Get a Title Company that pays attention to detail.

- Get an experienced Title Attorney who will advise you on how you can save on fees and taxes.

- Get an Attorney who understands different types of entities that can be used to hold property.

- Get an Attorney who works fast and is responsive to your needs and questions.

- Mystery shop them to determine if the Staff is attentive and polite before you engage them for business.

Insurance Company

- Know all the Types of insurance available and what your Lender will require depending on the nature of your real estate acquisition.

- Know the Amount of Coverage needed.

- Get the Exact Wording of the Mortgagee Clause directly from the Lender's Attorney (who controls closing). They must be satisfied with it.

- Get an experienced Insurance Agent who will shop around and explain your options. Be persistent and attentive to this.

Surveyor

- Get the Survey from the Seller when buying any property with the proper legal description. This will save you time and money.

- Understand that problems with the legal description can cost time and money so get a handle on this upfront.

Architect

- Interview many Local Architects to determine who is proactive and creative and really interested in your project.

- Your architect must have connections and relationships in Zoning, Inspection and Building Departments. Don't bring in an architect who is not familiar with the area and doesn't have connections because it will delay your project in several ways when he needs to deal with local authorities.

- If your property is in a Historical District, your architect must understand the requirements of the City's Historical Commission. The Historical folks can put a damper on your project so be sure to find out what their requirements are sooner rather than later.

- Your Architect must provide professional detailed drawings.

- Your Architect must work well with your contractor and watch out for your interests by paying attention to every wall, every ceiling and every floor in every room to make sure things are done well and up to code.

- A great architect will research and ask questions for you to find out whatever is necessary to make your project successful and ultimately approved by city inspectors.

- A great architect will look ahead and use his/her vision and expertise in design to make sure the layout of your project is done in the best way possible.

Lender's Attorney

- They work for the Lender and control whether or not you will get to closing.

- The Lender's Attorney creates the Closing Checklist so make sure you get a copy for yourself to see what they require instead of waiting for your attorney or Lender Representative to get it to you.

- You pay for your Lender's Attorney so make sure you know their fee upfront and how they bill so that you can watch how they bill for time.

Inspection

- Find out if Oil tank, Termite and Environmental Inspections need to be done sooner rather than later or else these can delay your closing.

- Find out if there are any Tax Credits and what the requirements are to apply for them.

Your Real Estate Attorney

- Shop around and ask other investors to recommend a real estate attorney experienced with the type of real estate you are buying.

- Make sure your attorney is not wimpy and will fight for you and be proactive in making suggestions about the clauses in your legal agreements. You must make sure your attorney is worth his salt and will get tough when necessary. You don't want someone who is all talk and no balls when it comes to dealing with Opposing Counsel.

- Get an attorney who is willing to change the paperwork and add valuable terms that are in your best interest.

- Get an Attorney who has local connections in city government and can get things done fast.

- Know your attorney's fee upfront and how they bill you for time. Don't allow them to store up invoices and then give you a shocking bill at the end. Keep track of their billings.

- Pay attention to how responsive their support staff is when you first interview them. You will be dealing with these people over a long period of time and must feel comfortable doing so.

- Find out what modes of communication they use: Email, Voicemail, Fax, Mail?

- Make sure that your attorney always seems to be working in your best interest. If you ever get the feeling that he or she is just pushing paper, get rid of them fast! Your deals are too important to be taken for granted.

Condo Attorney

- If you are dealing with condominiums, make sure you get an attorney who is experienced in preparing Condo Documents as there are a lot of nuisances to condo ownership.

Realtors/ Real Estate Brokers

- Identify several to find out who is really knowledgeable and experienced in the local market.

- Pay attention to whether or not they have a Sense of Urgency, are interested in your property and knows how to do all types of Marketing – not just the run of the mill marketing.

- Make sure they know how to qualify buyers or tenant buyers upfront before wasting your precious time.

- Pay attention to how aggressive and creative they are and whether or not they are also investors themselves. If your realtor is creative and flexible it makes it easier for you to structure a creative deal with the other party. Take time to find the creative, enthusiastic agent who thinks out of the box.

- Make sure your Realtor provides accurate information to buyers and tenants in writing upfront so that there are no misunderstandings.

Taxes

- If selling your property, understand Sections 1031 and 121 of the tax code. It is critical to understand the tax implications of your sale.

Liens

- Find out about any Liens upfront from your Title Company. This will help you structure or renegotiate your offer or deal.

Entities

- Since you should not be purchasing in your own name, be sure to have an entity created and have your Articles of Formation and Operating Agreements done.

- You will also need to have an idea of Other Principals involved in your transaction who will be on the paperwork.

Documents

- Read every word yourself and don't hesitate to change something or negotiate something in your favor. Never scan a legal document and sign it. Read every word and if you don't understand something, ask and get an explanation before signing.

Fees Charged

- Understand how to read the HUD or Closing Statement because every line item is coming out of someone's pocket, likely yours. Also, it is normal to have errors on a closing statement so you need to pay attention to every line item.

- Find out about Recording fees and how you may be able to save on them.

Interest Calculations

- Calculate interest yourself to make sure it was done properly.

How to be prepared and be in control of getting to closing.

- Note deadlines and don't hesitate to call folks to follow-up. Be a nag if necessary.

- Be very specific in questioning all parties about what needs to be done.

- The Attorneys on both sides rule in terms of getting to the closing table so know who they are and get the word from them directly if necessary on what's next.

Setting Expectations & Ground Rules with Everyone Involved.

- Be tough and demanding upfront

- Most of these people have jobs and are not investors, entrepreneurs or business owners. Therefore they have no clue about the value of time or money.

- Allow time to review documents carefully with your attorney, including the HUD (Closing) statement.

- If you don't have to go to the closing and can review docs prior then do so. It minimizes the opportunity for the other party to try to renegotiate at the closing table.

- You may give someone else Power of Attorney in your absence.

- Always have a "Time is of the Essence" clause.

- Again, always have competent, experienced Legal Representation and always keep them on their toes.

Cost of a closing

- Understand all the costs involved when Buying, doing Construction or Rehab, and Selling, before getting too deep in any deal.

Post Closing Documents

- If you are eager to close, find out what can be provided after closing that is not critical to getting the closing done.

- Keep all documents in order for when you go to sell later or for tax purposes.

Private Lenders, Alternatives to Institutions

- Private Lenders, especially in these times are the way to go to get your deals done.

- Only deal with accredited and savvy lenders. You don't want to work with someone who will need their money back next week or be a pain or a nuisance to you. You want someone who is easy to work with and has some investing and business savvy, and will be happy with the return on investment they get from you.

- Find out who has extra money available to lend or invest with you and who may have a Self-Directed IRA with idle funds.

- Be sure to take great care of your private lenders by over-communicating with them as they are much better to deal with than institutional lenders. If they enjoy doing one deal with you they will likely spread the word and help you fund other deals.

Rules to live by

- Time is your most valuable asset

- Assume that everybody is incompetent. Don't trust anyone and assume they know what they are doing.

- Ask lots of questions and get timeframes and commitments in writing.

- Keep a paper trail via fax or email with dates and times. No verbals. After conversation, send a note of understanding to document the conversation.

- No one cares as much as you because it's not their money or asset.

- Everybody lies some of the time.

- Everyone is willing to spend your money because it's not theirs.

- Pay attention to details. Keep your Eyes Open and Don't blink.

- Never accept the short answer: NO. Delve and ask why. Challenge everyone for solutions and alternatives. Find the experts and professionals who can explain things and come up with creative solutions.

- Don't ever work with people who are drones and don't think or offer solutions.

- Only deal with experienced, interested professionals who are happy to help your project be a success.

- Don't allow anyone to learn on your time or dime.

- Fire fast and hire slowly.

- You won't get in too deep to find out that you may have a bad deal if you ask upfront for all that is required and do upfront due diligence.

- Put demands on lenders, both institutional and private to deliver or back off. Time is of the Essence clause is required in all that you do.

- Everything is negotiable. Never accept the first number.

- Cast a wide net and shop around for private lenders and attorneys.

- Never allow any professional to feel that they are in charge. Always remember that you are the client and it's your money.

- Don't assume that any of these service providers really care about hurrying to get paid. It's just a job for them that they do everyday in most cases.

- Stay away from those service providers where you can't get a hold of them, they give you wrong information, and their staff is rude or unresponsive.

- In all you do, speak up, be pushy, be persistent, be aggressive, be vocal, and be inquisitive, always with a sense of urgency. Your money and your time depend on it, even if some may not like you and call you an SOB!

Marlene's 15 Guiding Principles for A Lifetime in Business

Nothing but your own thoughts can dampen your progress – control your thoughts and you control your life — *Anonymous*

I will leave you with 15 Guiding Principles for A Lifetime in Business to deal with getting screwed and to avoid getting screwed no matter what type of business you are in:

1. Remember that ALL successful business owners and entrepreneurs have attended the School of Hard Knocks, without exception! Make it a point to study the "behind the scenes" of their business operations, how they think, how they live, how they market, how they manage their money, how they deal with the people around them, and their philosophies about business and life. Model those things that you find most admirable in their life stories.

2. Stay laser focused on acquiring and building profit-

able assets that throw off enough cash to take care of you, your family and your lifestyle. Then make sure you ruthlessly protect your assets from predators.... and your possible carelessness.

3.   Do All Things on Purpose and Be Strategic. Think and Plan your Moves Many Steps Ahead of Your Opponents and Competition. Take an Honest Look at what's ahead for you so that you can be proactive and not reactive.

4.   In all that you do Track and Measure Activities so that you always know your numbers and can keep score. If you don't know your numbers, you are destined for failure and loss!

5.   Conduct business and live life on your own terms. Get clarity on what works and does not work for you then set your own ground rules and policies for how you do business with everyone. If others can't conform, simply don't do business with them.

6.   Never trust blindly. Always do your research and thorough due diligence, and always inspect what you expect to happen by having ongoing checks and balances in place. Having done research you can take calculated

risks instead of throwing caution to the wind. Don't be shy about asking tough and challenging questions of everyone around you!

7.   Deal swiftly on the offensive with your enemies and detractors because they can and will do too much damage to you, your business interests, and your loved ones.

8.   Always take very good care of those who take care of you. Never take them for granted.

9.   Understand that many people around you are looking for a handout and a free and easy ride on your dime. They have the mentality of entitlement. Later for hard work and earning their own way! That said, only reward people for results, performance and actions taken...not just because they showed up with hands stretched out. In business and life, you should not get compensated for attendance.

10.   Choose very carefully who you associate it. Seek to associate only with those who wish you well, those who operate with honesty and integrity, those who support you wholeheartedly, and those who are smarter than you (because you will always learn much from them).

Note the "return on investment" on whom you spend your time with and what you give your attention to.

11. Study closely how others leverage other people's money, other people's customers, other people's resources and other people's time. Learn to master the art of leverage especially when you have little or no money, no customers, no staff, and little or no time to get things done. It starts with figuring out what you have to offer that is of value to others. This includes your experience, knowledge and expertise. With this mindset and approach you can work on striking creative deals to get things done and create great value for others. Bottom line: learn how to make money without money. The place to start is to study the activities of self-made millionaire entrepreneurs and creative real estate investors.

12. Never get too comfortable or take things for granted in life. Things can very quickly take a turn for the worst and you can lose it all very quickly.

13. Take Inventory of what you have to work with and your knowledge base, Get your Priorities Straight and Focus on What Really Matters NOW and what you can do NOW.

14. Always have a Plan B, Plan C, Plan D, and more in all that you do. Many times Plan A does not work out as you planned!

15. Most importantly, whenever you get knocked down, ALWAYS get back up. Your Positive Attitude, Resilience and Persistence are the keys to making a comeback and staying in the game. Success is the Best Revenge!

Epilogue

*Regret is the most useless emotion there is. It does
absolutely nothing for anyone — Anonymous*

I know you must have related to a couple of these harsh
lessons learned and perhaps they brought back unpleasant
memories. Never mind! Put it all behind you, enjoy the present
moment, and look to paint a bright and exciting future.

Most importantly, I want you to understand that you are
not alone and that you are in the majority as there is a lot of
screwing going on in business these days! I encourage you to
start a dialog with your wise mentors and advisors and other
business owners to help you find solutions to your problems
as opposed to suffering in silence or from embarrassment. ☺

I encourage you to continue on your business journey and
never give up despite the setbacks and challenges you have
faced and will likely face in the future. In business and real
estate there is never a dull moment and things don't always
go smoothly!

The key is to Never Quit and Throw in the Towel when it
comes to achieving your life and business goals. Remember,

we only have this one life to live and we are not getting out of it alive!

Keep pressing forward and heed the lessons learned along the way. You will have failures and must learn from them. We all have failures and failures are really the best teachers. Don't ever be afraid of Failure!

Most of all, heed the wisdom of others who have gone before you and try your best NOT TO GET SCREWED!

I will leave you with one of my favorite quotes from Teddy Roosevelt...

THE MAN IN THE ARENA – THEODORE ROOSEVELT

"It is not the critic who counts; not the man who points out how the strong man stumbles, or where the doer of deeds could have done them better. The credit belongs to the man who is actually in the arena, whose face is marred by dust and sweat and blood; who strives valiantly; who errs, who comes short again and again, because there is no effort without error and shortcoming; but who does actually strive to do the deeds; who knows great enthusiasms, the great devotions; who spends himself in a worthy cause; who at the best knows in the end the triumph of high achievement, and who at the worst, if he fails, at least fails while daring greatly, so that his place shall never be with those cold and timid souls who neither know victory nor defeat."

47 Books From Marlene Green's Personal Library That You Must Read To Help You Avoid Or Deal With Getting Screwed In Business

Success is hastened or delayed by ones' habits
— Anonymous

1. Mean Business: How I Save Bad Companies and Make Good Companies Great by Albert J. Dunlap

2. No B.S. Ruthless Management of People & Profits by Dan Kennedy

3. No B.S. Business Success by Dan Kennedy

4. The Knack: How Street-Smart Entrepreneurs Learn To Handle Whatever Comes Up by Norm Brodsky and Bo Burlingham

5. People Get Screwed All The Time by Robert Massi, Esq.

6.   They Went Broke?! Bankruptcies and Money Disasters of the Rich and Famous by Roland Gary Jones, Esq.

7.   The Complete Book of Greed by M. Hirsh Goldberg

8.   The Prince by Niccolo Machiavelli

9.   The 48 Laws of Power by Robert Greene

10. Thick Face, Black Heart by Chin-Ning Chu

11. When Bad Things Happen to Good People by Harold S. Kushner

12. Management Mess-Ups by Mark Eppler

13. The Top Ten Mistakes Leaders Make by Hans Finzel

14. The First Billion is the Hardest by T. Boone Pickens

15. How to Spot a Liar: Why People Don't Tell the Truth and How You Can Catch Them by Gregory Hartley and Maryann Karinch

16. The Billion Dollar BET: Robert Johnson and the Inside Story of Black Entertainment Television by Brett Pulley

17. Succeeding Against the Odds: The Autobiography of a Great American Businessman by John H. Johnson with Lerone Bennett Jr.

18. Confessions of an S.O.B by Al Neuharth (Founder of USA Today)

19. Think Big and Kick Ass by Donald Trump

20. The Art of The Comeback by Donald Trump

21. The Art of The Deal by Donald Trump

22. Trump Style Negotiation by George Ross

23. Founders At Work: Stories of Startups' Early Days by Jessica Livingston

24. How to Be A Billionaire: Proven Strategies From the Titans of Wealth by Martin Fridson

25. Diary of a Small Business Owner: A Personal Account of How I Built a Profitable Business by Anita Brattina

26. Burst This! by Frank McKinney

27. The Tap by Frank McKinney

28. Good to Great by Jim Collins

29. Built to Last by Jim Collins

30. Mastering the Rockefeller Habits by Verne Harnish

31. Psycho-Cybernetics by Dr. Maxwell Maltz

32. Woulda, Coulda, Shoulda: Overcoming Regrets, Mistakes and Missed Opportunities by Dr. Arthur Freeman & Rose DeWolf

33. Power and Persuasion by Michael Masterson

34. Reading People: How to Understand People and Predict Their Behavior – Anytime, Anyplace by Dr. Jo-Ellan Dimitrius & Wendy Patrick Mazzarella

35. The Definitive Book of Body Language by Allan and Barbara Pease

36. The Power of Focus by Jack Canfield, Mark Victor Hansen & Les Hewitt

37. Worry by Dr. Edward Hallowell

Additional Resources Recommended by Marlene Green That Will Help You Tremendously

Visit www.ScrewedInBusiness.com to share your thoughts about this book, how you have been screwed in business (by partners, by professionals, by contractors, or by tenants) and what lessons you have learned that you would like to share with others. I would love to hear from you so please also share with me how this book and the information provided has touched your life.

Visit www.MarleneRecommends.com to get Marlene Green's Personal Recommendations on Tools and Educational Resources that will help you no matter what your level of experience is in business or what business you are in.

Visit www.MillionaireBlueprints.com to get your copy of Millionaire Blueprints Magazine and become a Member of the Millionaire Blueprints community by stepping into the Millionaire Blueprints Arena!

For your Conference, Retreat, Organization or School, you are welcome to invite Marlene Green to be a Guest Speaker or Panelist at your next Live Event or Teleseminar Event. Ms. Green is also available for Media Interviews and Commentary.

For the most up to date Contact Information for Marlene Green, simply visit www.MarleneGreen.com.

Interested in Becoming a Millionaire Blueprints™ Strategic Partner?

Millionaire Blueprints Media LLC is on a mission to promote entrepreneurship and business education in grades K through 12, and small business growth and prosperity on Main Street.

We are passionate about sharing 'how to' information, valuable tools, and educational resources *directly from self-made millionaires* chosen to be profiled in our various forms of media for the benefit of our audience members.

Millionaire Blueprints™ Strategic Partners are businesses that support our mission and are committed to providing information, tools and resources that will truly help our audience members pursue their business, entrepreneurial, wealth and personal development goals. In turn, we encourage our audience members to work with our Strategic Partners and extract value from what they have to offer to improve their personal and business lives.

Because we value our relationship with our audience, we have an evaluation process for which businesses can be designated a Strategic Partner.

If you are interested in learning more about the **Millionaire Blueprints™ Strategic Partner Program**, the benefits, and the application process, please send a request to our Help Desk at www.MBMHelpDesk.com with the subject line, "Strategic Partners" and a team member will follow up with you promptly.

A Part of the Proceeds from Book Sales will benefit Marlene Green's favorite not for profit organizations because she believes very much in their Founders' Missions to Make a Difference.

Marlene Green encourages you to visit their websites and use "Your Time, Talent or Treasure" (as stated by Frank McKinney) to Support These Phenomenal Organizations that Positively Impact and Empower Lives in the United States and Abroad in so many ways!

$ Scott Sullivan's Caring 4 Kids Foundation, www.Caring4KidsFoundation.org

$ Alex Ellis' Tied to Greatness, www.TiedToGreatness.org

$ Sabrina Lamb's World Of Money, www.WorldOfMoney.org

$ Frank McKinney's Caring House Project Foundation, www.CHPF.org

$ Kiva.org, www.Kiva.org,

$ Amber Lupton & Nathan Otto's P:5Y, www.P5Y.org,

$ Scott Harrison's Charity Water, www.CharityWater.org

Visit www.ScrewedInBusiness.com to be notified about Marlene's other offerings including: **"How We Got Screwed in Business: Real Life Stories of People Just Like You Who Got Screwed in Business"**

To Place an Order for More Copies of Screwed In Business! & To Learn about Special Quantity Discounts for your Group or Organization, visit www.ScrewedInBusiness.com

Five Important Things You Should Do Now To Improve Your Business, Help Your Friends & Others Who May Be Getting Screwed Right Now, And Minimize YOUR Chances Of Getting Screwed In Business...

1. Share your AH-Hahs from reading this book and your stories and the harsh lessons you have learned in business with us. Start by registering your book with us at www.ScrewedInBusiness.com so you can stay in touch with us and receive updates on other Screwed In Business™ books and related offerings! You will receive a special gift as a thank you.

2. Share *Screwed In Business* with your friends or encourage them to get their own copies. Also, give *Screwed In Business* as a gift to other business owners you know. *Remember, part of the proceeds go to support charities that are making a difference*!

3. Share your Video Review or Written Review for *Screwed In Business* on Amazon.com.

4. Schedule time to read and learn from the books on *Marlene Green's Recommended Reading List*. If necessary, borrow them from your local library!

Visit the author's affiliated websites to get more useful resources and valuable information that will help you in your business:
www.MarleneRecommends.com
www.MillionaireBlueprints.com

5.   Visit the following valuable links now for the special bonus offers for:

Millionaire Blueprints Magazine,
www.ScrewedInBusiness.com/MBPMag

Information Marketing Association,
www.ScrewedInBusiness.com/IMA

The Most Incredible FREE Gift Ever from Dan Kennedy, www.ScrewedInBusiness.com/GKIC

About the Author

M arlene Green, Entrepreneur, Speaker, Real Estate Investor, Consultant and Business Strategist, is President and CEO of Millionaire Blueprints Media LLC (www.MillionaireBlueprints.com), home of the award-winning national magazine, Millionaire Blueprints Magazine.

She is also the Chapter Director of Glazer-Kennedy Insider's Circle's Manhattan and Northern New Jersey Chapters (www.GKICNewYork.com). Glazer-Kennedy Insider's Circle, founded by marketing gurus Dan Kennedy and Bill Glazer, is a diverse international organization of entrepreneurs, business owners and direct response marketers committed to seeking fast and dramatic growth and greater control, independence and security in their business and personal lives.

Marlene is a master networker and connector who enjoys providing 'fresh eyes' and connecting the dots for her audience, friends, members and clients. She is a passionate crusader for the "Lonely Entrepreneur" and encourages you to join a mastermind group of smart, like-minded people where ideas and strategies in wealth-building, marketing, business and life management are discussed for everyone's benefit. Marlene is a co-author of the "Secrets of Peak Performers" book with Dan Kennedy, Bill Glazer and Lee Milteer and is featured in Dan Kennedy's book "The Phenomenon: Achieve More in the next 12 Months than the Previous 12 Years".

'Seen and Heard Everywhere', Marlene confesses to being a seminar junkie and values learning from THE BEST teachers in real estate, business, and marketing. She operates on the Principle of Gaining a Slight Edge by embracing lifelong learning. Marlene understands The "Missed Opportunity" Cost of Ignorance as there was a time when she had zero direct access to millionaire mentors and teachers who would share their wisdom and blueprints that when implemented would help her leapfrog to prosperity.

As President and CEO of Millionaire Blueprints Media, and with the contribution of members of the Millionaire Blueprints' Founders Circle, the Millionaire Blueprints' Society of Millionaires, the Implementation Team, and the Strategic Partners at Millionaire Blueprints Media, Marlene is committed to delivering the Blueprints: "Detailed Examples and Step by Step Instructions from Self-Made Millionaires", that Millionaire Blueprints Magazine is known for to every corner of the world.

Marlene graduated from New York University's Stern School of Business and spent ten years as a corporate and legal technology consultant for the top 50 law firms and Fortune 100 companies. She has traveled extensively throughout the United States, Europe, Africa, Asia, The Caribbean, South America and Australia. Marlene grew up in Kingston, Jamaica and is quite proud of her Jamaican heritage.

Printed in the United States
221766BV00004B/4/P

9 780981 827407